MOUNTAINS

of the Pharaohs

The Untold Story

of the

Pyramid Builders

DOUBLEDAY

New York   London

Toronto   Sydney   Auckland

MOUNTAINS
of the Pharaohs

ZAHI HAWASS

PUBLISHED BY DOUBLEDAY
a division of Random House, Inc.

DOUBLEDAY and the portrayal of an anchor with a dolphin are
registered trademarks of Random House, Inc.

www.doubleday.com

Book design by Donna Sinisgalli

Cataloging-in-Publication Data is on file with the Library of Congress.

ISBN-13: 978-0-385-50305-1
ISBN-10: 0-385-50305-9

First Edition

1 3 5 7 9 10 8 6 4 2

For David O'Connor

Contents

Introduction   *1*

Part One — The Dawn of the 4th Dynasty

CHAPTER ONE   The Reign of Sneferu   *13*

CHAPTER TWO   Sneferu at Meidum   *21*

CHAPTER THREE   Dahshur: Sneferu and the Cult of the Sun   *32*

CHAPTER FOUR   The Court of Sneferu   *42*

CHAPTER FIVE   The King Is Dead   *48*

Part Two — The Reign of the Sun God

CHAPTER SIX   The Early Reign of Khufu   *55*

CHAPTER SEVEN   Revolution in Year Five   *67*

CHAPTER EIGHT   Ruthless Monarch or Great Scientist?   *80*

CHAPTER NINE   Khufu's Court   *85*

CHAPTER TEN   The Completion of the Great Pyramid and the Death of Khufu   *101*

Part Three ~ The Heirs of Khufu

CHAPTER ELEVEN   Battles Stir Within the Royal Family:
                 Djedefre at Abu Rawash   *109*

CHAPTER TWELVE   The Conspiracies of Khafre   *114*

CHAPTER THIRTEEN   The Pyramid Complex of Khafre   *117*

CHAPTER FOURTEEN   The Court of Khafre   *133*

CHAPTER FIFTEEN   The Death of Khafre   *138*

CHAPTER SIXTEEN   Menkaure Ascends the Throne   *140*

Part Four ~ The Pyramid Builders at Giza

CHAPTER SEVENTEEN   The Pyramid Builders of Giza   *157*

CHAPTER EIGHTEEN   The Lives of the Pyramid Builders   *167*

Part Five ~ The End of an Era

CHAPTER NINETEEN   Shepseskaf, the Good Son   *179*

CHAPTER TWENTY   The Rising of the Sons of Re: The
                 Reign of Khentkawes and the Dawn of
                 the 5th Dynasty   *182*

CHAPTER TWENTY-ONE   The Abandonment of Giza   *185*

Conclusion   *194*

Acknowledgments   *197*

Bibliography   *199*

Index   *207*

MOUNTAINS

of the Pharaohs

Introduction

The year is c. 2609 B.C. Looking back across the sands of time, we can see the newly crowned king, Khufu, accompanied by his chief architect, Hemiunu, high on the empty, windswept expanse of the Giza Plateau. They stand together, a little distance from the large retinue of personal attendants that accompany them wherever they go, and take in the vista that surrounds them. To the west, stretching to the horizon where the sun god dies each night, is the golden yellow of the high desert savanna, still teeming with wild animals to be hunted. To the south, far in the distance, is the Step Pyramid of King Djoser, who ruled three-quarters of a century before and inaugurated the era of monumental building in stone to which they are now heir. Farther to the south, dwarfed by distance, are three of the pyramids built by Khufu's father, the great King Sneferu.

At the foot of the plateau to the east is a narrow band of low desert bordering the sudden and intense green of the floodplain. Through this runs the wide, silver-blue ribbon of the Nile. Far in the distance is the eastern horizon, where the sun is reborn each morning. This is the perfect place, Khufu decides, standing on the spot where his pyramid will rise over the course of the next two decades. The bedrock is

solid, good-quality limestone, covered only by a thin layer of the sand that blows in

from the west. A suitable quarry can be opened several hundred meters to the south

to provide stone for his monument, and the Nile is close enough to the foot of the

plateau so that more exotic materials can be brought in easily by boat through

the canals and harbors they will dig. This will be the biggest pyramid ever built, a

monument that will stand for eternity, a mountain of stone to ensure forever both

his own memory and the proper functioning of the Egyptian universe. And the

floodplain below is a perfect place for his palace and administrative city. The workers

and their overseers can be housed to the southeast, near the only major monument

already gracing the plateau, the low mud-brick tomb of one of Khufu's distant

ancestors. There is room nearby for the pyramid of his son and perhaps for the

monument of his son's son. This is it, the place where he will spend eternity.

Of course, this scene is imaginary. We don't really know how and when Khufu first came to Giza and chose it for his eternal home. We don't know who would have come with him or even if he himself would have walked around the site, since it is possible that he was carried whenever he went outside. We don't know for certain how old he was when he became king, although we can make a good guess. We don't even know what he looked like—the only certain image we have of him is a small ivory statuette. But we do know a great deal about the world he lived in (although we must view everything we find through the veils of time), and we are discovering more through the exciting excavations currently under way at Giza. We know the names and titles of many of the members of his family and of the people who inhabited his court. We know how his administration was structured and how the basic system of his government worked. We know a great deal about how Khufu's pyramid was built and why, and are now finding out about the people who actually dragged the great stones into place.

The Giza pyramids have fascinated humankind for millennia, ever since they were built. The Great Pyramid of Khufu itself is the most famous monument in the world, and it has been visited, measured, photographed, and studied by scholars and by enthusiasts for centuries. There are countless theories as to its construction and function; it has served us for millennia as an icon of stability and permanence and even as a symbol of magic. The Great Sphinx, carved by Khufu's son Khafre from an outcropping of rock in the low desert east of the plateau, has been the subject of enormous amounts of speculation and also a great deal of careful scientific study.

The pyramid complexes at Giza and the cults they housed were abandoned sometime within the five hundred years following their construction. The royal tombs themselves were robbed, although we do not know exactly when, by people who seemed to know what they were doing. The temple complexes surrounding them were vandalized, the walls stripped of their reliefs, and many of the statues smashed to provide materials for later cults. We recently discovered an unfinished statue of Rameses the Great, who ruled from about 1304 to 1237 B.C., carved out of a block of red granite that had been used as casing in the complex of Khufu's grandson Menkaure. Thus the pyramids were used as quarries by the descendants of their builders and continued to be gradually robbed of their stone over the millennia.

The pyramids, and especially the Sphinx, were the focus of various cults during the later pharaonic period. King Amenhotep II (c. 1459–1419 B.C.) erected a temple to the Sphinx on higher ground to the north. His son, Thutmose IV, whose claim to the monarchy seems to have been a bit shaky, set up his own stele (carved on a stone from one of the original temples at Giza) between the paws of the Sphinx. On it he tells the story of how, as a young prince, he had been hunting in the desert nearby and had fallen asleep in the shadow of this great beast, potent symbol of kingship throughout Egyptian history. The Sphinx had spoken, begging the prince to clear away the sand that now choked him up to his neck and promising in return the throne of Egypt. Both the prince and the Sphinx kept their promises—Thutmose IV cleared away the sand and did indeed become pharaoh. The cults at Giza were revived again later, during the 26th Dynasty (664–525 B.C.), when there were priests of the Giza pyramid builders and an active cult to the Sphinx itself.

Herodotus, the Greek traveler known as the "father of history," visited Giza during the fifth century B.C. and came home with all sorts of fantastic tales. Khufu was portrayed by him as a cruel, heartless ruler who used his subjects as slaves and even forced his own daughter into prostitution. By the Roman period (from 30 B.C. until the fourth century A.D.), Giza had become a tourist attraction. The Jewish historian Josephus, writing in the late first century A.D., first disseminated the persistent (and completely untrue) myth that the Hebrew slaves had worn themselves out building the pyramids.

By the end of the fourth century A.D., there was no one left who could read the ancient hieroglyphs. Myths and legends, already swirling around the massive monuments, multiplied and spread. The idea that the shape of the Great Pyramid served to keep metal from rusting, later expanded to include other magical preservative qualities, was first propounded by an Arab historian named al-Maqrizi in the fifteenth century A.D. (I have carried out my own experiment on this subject: I placed a pound of raw meat on a bookshelf in my office at Giza and a second pound in the burial chamber of Khufu's pyramid. I am sorry to report that the two samples decayed at the same rate and that it took several weeks for my office staff to recover completely from the smell. I will not be repeating this experiment.)

The Great Pyramid was first breached in relatively modern times by the Caliph al-Mamun. In around A.D. 820, he and his men either forced or, more likely, enlarged an entrance a little below and to one side of the original entrance in the north face, which had been closed and hidden completely by the ancient builders. It is not certain exactly what the caliph's men found: the most they may have discovered were some decayed bones inside Khufu's granite sarcophagus; ancient robbers had long ago taken away the treasures buried with the king. Unfortunately, although such bones would have been a great treasure for modern archaeologists, they were considered completely unimportant by the caliph and were discarded.

The casing stones covering the three pyramids, which would have given them a smooth-sided appearance very different from what we see today, were still relatively intact in the early twelfth century A.D. But the modern city of Cairo was thirsty for building material, and the casings of the pyramids and their temples were almost completely stripped between this time and the late nineteenth century.

European visitors began to add Giza to their itineraries in the twelfth century A.D., and for five centuries a slow but steady stream of travelers came to gaze upon the pyramids and Sphinx. Many went home and wrote memoirs, often accompanied by at best inaccurate, at worst inadvertently humorous, sketches of the antiquities. The first modern scholar to visit Giza was John Greaves, a professor of astronomy at Oxford University in the mid-seventeenth century. He produced reasonably precise measurements and a detailed description and concluded, based on his study of classical sources, that the pyramids were tombs built to ensure the eternal survival of the souls of Cheops (Greek for Khufu), Chephren (Khafre), and Mycerinus (Menkaure). Benoît de Maillet, French consul-general to Egypt from 1692 to 1708, was fascinated by the pyramids and made excellent drawings of the passages and chambers within the Great Pyramid.

The next century saw a surge in the number of travelers who took it upon themselves to make accurate records of the monuments they visited. Some of their descriptions are not quite on target, and their artistic abilities were decidedly uneven, but the records they left are invaluable and often give us information about details that have since disappeared. The fledgling science of Egyptology was put on a whole new footing by Napoleon Bonaparte, who brought a team of 150 scientists and scholars with him on his great expedition to Egypt in 1798. These men spent three years documenting everything they could, including the ancient monuments then visible, and produced an enormous illustrated treatise called the *Description de l'Égypte*.

The Napoleonic expedition touched off a new surge of interest in ancient Egypt. This resulted on the positive side in a significant increase in the number of scholars who devoted themselves to the study of the ancient culture. This number included Jean-François Champollion, who brought the silent hieroglyphic writings back to life in 1822. On the negative side, collectors, both private and museum sponsored, acquired an insatiable hunger for antiquities, and the rape of the ancient monuments began in earnest. An orgy of destruction sent a steady stream of statues, mummies, reliefs that had been ripped from their tombs, and anything else that could be loaded onto a ship, back to Europe. The "excavators" who sent these materials back home, destroying important evidence in the process of removing them from their original contexts, were often the same scientists responsible for studying them and preserving them.

Egyptology was accompanied at its birth by a dark twin, which we now refer to politely as pyramidology. Mystics and pseudoscientists began to come up with all sorts of far-fetched theories, sometimes based on coincidence and sometimes completely made up, to explain the pyramids. One of the first was John Taylor, who claimed in 1859 that the Great Pyramid was a "record of the measure of the Earth," and believed that the Egyptians knew the value of pi. He was followed by Charles Piazzi Smyth, who thought that the Great Pyramid was a scale model of the earth's circumference, built using a unit called the pyramid inch. He also believed that the interior chambers and passages of this monument had embedded in their measurements prophetic messages about important future events, left there by the lost tribe of Israel (who were also the ancestors, somehow, of the British).

One of Smyth's disciples was a young man named William Flinders Petrie, who came to Giza in 1880 to remeasure the Great Pyramid. His meticulous work disproved Smyth's theories beyond a doubt, and he left pyramidology to embrace the field of Egyptology. He carried out numerous rigorously scientific excavations, inventing and refining a new methodology as he worked, which formed the basis for the new discipline of archaeology. His excellent studies of the Giza pyramids are still useful today.

Petrie was followed at Giza by a number of scientific expeditions, most notably the Americans under George Reisner, the Germans and Austrians under Uvo Hölscher, Georg Steindorff, and Hermann Junker, and the Egyptians under Selim Hassan. These men carried out explorations of the three pyramids, their temple complexes, and the many tombs of officials and priests that surround them.

I am proud to be the heir of these great archaeologists. I have been working steadily at Giza since 1987 and have made many wonderful discoveries. Most of these have come about as a result of my site-management program, which I have instituted for the long-term safety and preservation of the ancient monuments. One of the achievements of which I am most proud is the Sphinx Conservation Project, a decade-long effort to restore and preserve the Great Sphinx, which we completed in 1997.

Working with and alongside me has been an American Egyptologist named Mark Lehner. Over the course of the last decade we have begun to uncover the remains of the pyramid builders, shedding important new light on the history of the Old Kingdom. I am now excavating the cemeteries where the workers who dragged the stones, their supervisors, and the artisans and minor officials who formed part of the royal staff were buried. These people were not foreign slaves; they were native

Egyptians who toiled voluntarily in the service of their god-kings. Mark is uncovering the area where food and tools for the workers were produced and is now finding parts of a settlement, glimpses of which we had seen in earlier soundings under the modern village nearby.

The pyramids and their attendant Sphinx at Giza are often taken out of context, treated as if they had appeared magically and stand alone. In fact, they are only three of over thirty major pyramids that line the edge of the high desert to the west of the Nile near modern Cairo. They are the culmination of a long sequence of development that began hundreds of years earlier with the tombs of the earliest kings and princes of Egypt and accelerated rapidly during the century before the reign of Khufu.

By piecing together our bits of evidence—tombs, texts, reliefs, bones, and everyday objects—we can create a picture of the world of the great pyramid builders. There will be large gaps and faint places, and even outright mistakes that will be corrected as more evidence emerges from the sands of Egypt, but our picture is already full and vibrant. I must warn you now that there will be no aliens, no mysterious people from Atlantis, in this world. We will use only real evidence to paint our picture, not the nonsense on which the theories that attribute the pyramids to magical powers and outside forces are based. The pyramids were built by native Egyptians in the third millennium B.C. by the very men and women whose bones we are now finding in the sands nearby. Scholars may argue about the details, but the basic facts are irrefutable.

The history of the Giza pyramids begins three-quarters of a century before our King Khufu takes the throne. Between c. 2687 and 2668 B.C., a king named Netjerikhet (known to us as Djoser) built the first large-scale monument in stone, the Step Pyramid at Saqqara. His immediate successors attempted to follow his example, and did some experimentation of their own, but none lived long enough to complete his own monument or make serious technical progress, until the reign of a king named Sneferu.

Sneferu was the first king of a new dynasty, the 4th. He ruled for at least twenty-four years, possibly as many as fifty-four, and left behind three great monuments, which included the first straight-sided, or true, pyramids. He was succeeded by his son Khufu, who stands at the center of our story. Khufu ruled during a time when Egypt was strong and united under the powerful central administration that his predecessors' massive building projects had helped to create. His Great Pyramid at Giza was the culmination of the work of his father; after building three great pyramids, the royal architects and engineers had learned an enormous amount, and he benefited from their expertise.

Khufu ruled for thirty-two years, and was succeeded by one of his sons. This king, Djedefre, left Giza for the nearby site of Abu Rawash, where he planned his own smaller pyramid. He died only eight years later and left his eternal home unfinished. It was then the turn of Khafre, another son of Khufu, to take the reins of government. He came back to Giza and built his own pyramid next to his father's, slightly smaller but standing on a rise so that it looks just as tall. It was his men who carved the Sphinx out of the rocky outcrop that guards the plateau, fashioning it into an image of a recumbent lion with the head of a king.

Khafre ruled for about thirty years, and the bureaucracy that ran the country grew ever larger and more efficient. An ephemeral king, whom we know as Bicheris (in Greek) or Baka, may have ruled after him for about four years; this king is left out of most king lists and neglected in most discussions of Old Kingdom history. There is also a remote possibility that yet another son of Khufu, Djedefhor, reigned for a short time. The next important king, Khafre's son Menkaure, stayed at Giza, choosing to build a smaller pyramid from more expensive materials rather than trying to match his father's and grandfather's grandeur of scale on what little available space was left on the plateau. But he died after twenty-four years on the throne, before the work was completed, and his son

Shepseskaf finished his monument in mud brick before he himself moved to Saqqara, about nine kilometers (about five and a half miles) to the south.

Shepseskaf ruled for only about four years and built a large mastaba, a low rectangular tomb, rather than a pyramid. The last ruler of the 4th Dynasty, a queen named Khentkawes (c. 2519–2513 B.C.), returned to Giza to build a massive tomb, but this was the last great monument built here. Afterward, the site was abandoned in favor of other pyramid fields to the south, although its royal cults continued to flourish for hundreds of years.

Giza was the heart of Egypt for three generations. It was here that the royal government sat, where the court of the king spent much of its time. Raw materials, food, and cheap labor from all over the country poured onto its shores to expedite the building of eternal temples to the god-kings. But our story begins in the court of Sneferu at Meidum, where Khufu was born and learned to be a king.

Part One

The Dawn of
the 4th Dynasty

Chapter One

The Reign of Sneferu

King Sneferu was very pleased. His brother Rahotep, an energetic, handsome young man with black hair and a debonair mustache, had returned from his raid across the southern border into Nubia laden with booty. The Nubians had put up very little fight and surrendered with hardly any bloodshed. The might of the Egyptian king was already a legend in foreign lands; and the arrival of his well-trained troops, breaching the rocky impassability of the First Cataract with speed and efficiency, had struck fear into the hearts of the enemy. Seven thousand healthy men and women had surrendered themselves and two hundred thousand head of precious cattle to the royal expedition; these families would be put to work tilling the royal estates scattered up and down the river Nile, tending the royal herds, and helping to build the royal monuments. Sneferu was so pleased with his young brother that he ordered the royal sculptors to carve exquisite statues of the prince and his wife, the beautiful Nofret, out of fine limestone. Little did he dream that archaeologists would stumble across these same statues over four thousand years later or that the workman who first laid eyes on the lifelike painted faces of Rahotep and his wife, their eyes gleaming with inlaid crystal, would be so frightened that his heart would

stop forever.

Sneferu was a king revered throughout pharaonic history as a wise and beneficent ruler. He was one of the most powerful kings of ancient Egypt and the founder of a great dynasty; he ushered in a period of impressive achievement, an era of power and mystery. Sneferu was an energetic monarch who sent both trading and military expeditions into neighboring lands and carried out an ambitious building program within Egypt's borders, leaving behind no less than four pyramids. Given the name Ptah-Sneferu ("Ptah is the one who makes things beautiful"), he was remembered by later Egyptians as the archetype of an excellent king. He was held in such high honor that he was deified five hundred years after his death; his cult remained active for thousands of years.

Sneferu's mother was a queen named Mersyankh, the wife of Huni, the last king of the 3rd Dynasty. Since Sneferu was considered to have inaugurated a new dynasty, we believe that Mersyankh was not the principal wife of Huni but was instead a secondary queen. Huni and his principal queen, whose name we do not know, had a daughter named Hetepheres. If the main royal couple had any sons, they all must have died before their father. To ensure the line of succession, Huni married Sneferu to his half sister Hetepheres, and made him the new heir to the throne.

In ancient Egypt, queens—the king's chief wife, his mother, and sometimes his eldest daughter—symbolized the female principle and were essential to proper rule. Some of these queens exerted considerable authority and power of their own—we know of four queens dating from various periods of Egyptian history who actually ruled Egypt, even though this was contrary to the fundamental tenets of Egyptian kingship.

We do not truly understand the rules of succession in the Old Kingdom, although it is generally assumed that the next king should be the eldest son of the reigning king and his principal queen (although there is no particular evidence for this except the better-known practices of Middle and New Kingdom kings). I myself am not certain that the eldest son was supposed to inherit the throne, since we know of many kings' eldest sons who held important administrative titles but were never kings. In any case, when, for whatever reason, the successor was the son of a minor wife or came from a secondary branch of the royal family, his claim was usually consolidated by marriage to a royal daughter, especially a daughter of the chief wife. Often this would mean marrying a half sister or a niece, a common practice for the king.

Sometimes the king also married his full sister. The reasons for this are not clear. Perhaps it was in order to consolidate family power or, more likely, because there was a divine precedent for it in the marriages of divine siblings. Brother-sister marriages are quite common in Egyptian mythology. The earth god Geb married his sister Nut, the goddess of the sky, and their four children paired up with one another. Their son Osiris married his sister Isis, and the second son, Seth, married the second daughter, Nephthys.

The principal queen and the queen mother shared in the divinity of the king and also had important roles in the religious life of the country. While the king was associated with male images, such as the Horus falcon (a sky god) and the bull (a potent symbol of royal might), his queen was identified with the vulture goddess Nekhbet, the tutelary deity of Upper Egypt, and with the cow goddess Hathor, daughter of the sun god Re and protector of Horus. Thus, on one level, Huni was presumably maintaining the divine order by arranging the marriage of Sneferu as the future Horus king to his half sister Hetepheres as an incarnation of Hathor. On a more practical level, I am sure that all this served to keep power in the family.

Sneferu became king at the death of his father, in about 2649 B.C. When he first put on the double crown, symbol of a united nation,

Egypt was already a strong, wealthy state, secure within her own borders. Deserts formed a formidable barrier to the east and west; the Mediterranean Sea protected her northern border; and cataracts—outcroppings of granite—broke up the Nile to the south, making navigation difficult and protecting the Egyptian heartland from threats of invasion. During Sneferu's reign, Egypt became even more powerful, with access to enormous resources of goods and manpower.

The role of the king was central to Egyptian society as a whole. The worldview of the ancient Egyptians was based on an important philosophical concept called *ma'at*. This was represented by a feather, or by a goddess with a feather on her head, and translates roughly as "truth," or "justice." The broader and more accurate meaning of *ma'at* was the proper functioning of the cosmos, the way that things were supposed to be. The ideal Egyptian world was a place of stability and predictability, where the chaos of darkness and limitless water that both preceded and surrounded the cosmos was kept at bay by the eternal renewal of creation. This was played out on the earthly stage by the rising and setting of the sun each day, and echoed in many smaller ways. The fertility of the land was assured by the annual Nile flood and the predictable round of the seasons. Fields were prepared; crops were sown and harvested; domesticated animals were born, reared, and slaughtered; and the wild creatures that lived on the edges of the land—desert animals, fish, wild birds, and human foreigners—were all officially kept in check by the efforts of the royal house.

The king had the primary responsibility for the maintenance of *ma'at*. It was his job, as the earthly embodiment of the god Horus, to ensure that the world continued to function properly. We know that the god Horus, depicted as a hawk, was important from the earliest days of the Egyptian monarchy. An important myth, reconstructed from later sources, tells us that in the beginning of time, Horus was the son of the sun god Re and ruler of the sky. He had two eyes, the sun and the moon. An evil god named Seth wounded his moon eye, so that each month it would wane as it was damaged and wax as it was healed. According to another myth, Seth was the brother of Osiris, first king of Egypt. Seth was jealous of his brother and conspired to murder him, after which he cut his body into pieces, scattered them throughout the land, and took the throne. Osiris's sister wife, Isis, gathered the pieces together and wrapped them into the semblance of a body, and revived her husband long enough to conceive a child, Horus. Isis raised Horus in secret, and when he was old enough, she brought him to a council of the gods to reclaim his father's throne. After much back and forth and considerable nonfatal bloodshed, Horus reclaimed the throne and became king of Egypt, first of the northern part (Lower Egypt) and then of the entire land.

The king stood between the terrestrial realm and the celestial one and interceded with the gods on behalf of his subjects. Temple ritual was an important tool for the maintenance of *ma'at*. The king was, in theory, the chief priest in all of the temples; in a nation with no real division of church and state, this was not a small task. All his official activities, from military campaigns to building projects to holding court and carrying out ceremonies of various sorts, were in some way part of his effort to maintain the order of the universe. The name Sneferu took upon his ascension to the throne, Nebma'at, or Lord of *Ma'at*, reflects his concern with maintaining the proper order of the cosmos.

Despite its relative geographical isolation, Egypt in the early Old Kingdom was already carrying on a variety of relationships with her neighbors. To the northeast, the coast of what is now Syria and Israel was occupied by a number of fortified cities. Trading caravans traveled through the Sinai Peninsula, carrying exotic goods from afar; the Egyptians also exploited the turquoise and copper mines in the Sinai. To the west was the land of the Tgehenu, the Libyans, who seem mostly to have been treated by the Egyptians as marauding tribes who needed to be restrained.

The lands far to the south were of especial interest to the rulers of the Old Kingdom, as they were to later kings. Many wonderful and exotic goods, such as ebony and incense, exotic animals and their by-products—ivory, ostrich eggs, and panther skins, to name a few—came from this area, and the Egyptians were concerned with protecting their access to raw materials such as gold from the Nubian desert and diorite from mines to the southwest. Under Sneferu's energetic leadership, Egypt expanded her trading relationships with her neighbors and mounted a number of military expeditions into nearby territories.

Our knowledge of the primary events of Sneferu's reign comes from a fragmentary basalt stele called the Palermo Stone. This monument, which dates from the end of the 5th Dynasty, over two hundred years later, is the closest thing we have to a contemporary history of the 4th Dynasty. Its surface is divided into sections, each assigned to a specific king (listed in order from the beginning of Egyptian history and some way beyond, back into the mists of a mythical prehistory). Each section is divided into years, and within each year division is a list of the important events of that year; below the events is a record of the all-important level of the Nile flood. Unfortunately, only pieces of this important monument still survive, so many kings and many years have been lost to us. However, a segment of Sneferu's reign has been preserved, and it gives us a glimpse into some of the details of his reign.

In his thirteenth year as king, Sneferu launched a campaign into Nubia. Out of what must already have been a very small population, the expedition brought back seven thousand human prisoners and two hundred thousand head of cattle. Another campaign, in the eighteenth year of his reign, was against the Libyans to the west: the Egyptians brought back eleven thousand human prisoners and just over thirteen thousand head of cattle. To protect Egypt's borders from her enemies, Sneferu also built fortifications to the south and north. There are remains of an Old Kingdom town at the site of Buhen in northern Nubia that may indeed date back to Sneferu's reign; no archaeological remains of northern fortifications have been found.

The Sinai in the time of Sneferu was called "the land of turquoise." Inscriptions in the Wadi Maghara (located in southwest Sinai) bear testimony to military campaigns to the northeast. Reliefs carved into the cliffs of this remote locale show the king using his mace to smite the chieftain of the Bedouins, fighting to ensure the safety of the royal caravans and the mining expeditions. Sneferu's name was connected with the Sinai long after his death, and one of the mines at Wadi Maghara was named after him. He was deified here in the 12th Dynasty, six hundred years after his death.

Not all of the events known from Sneferu's reign were acts of war. Boatbuilding was important, which is not surprising given the importance of the Nile as the main route for transportation and trade. Some of the boats were also seagoing vessels, important for trading with the coastal cities in the eastern Mediterranean. The Palermo Stone entry for the thirteenth year records an expedition to Byblos, a vital port city on the coast of Lebanon, to bring back a special type of wood—probably cedar or some other coniferous wood (Egypt itself was and is relatively wood poor, and the types of trees that grew there, such as acacia and palm, were not suitable for many sorts of building activities); the boats used for this expedition would themselves have been made of imported wood. Sneferu used some cedar from Lebanon to build an enormous boat, over one hundred meters (328 feet) long. This was probably a state barge, used for royal journeys on the Nile. Sixty royal "sixteener" boats, possibly boats with sixteen oars, were also built in the same year. In the next year, three more large boats were built of various types of wood, and foreign wood was also used to make doors for the royal palace. Ancient cedar beams, perhaps even from this same shipment, were also found inside Sneferu's first pyramid at Dahshur, the Bent Pyramid.

In addition to these military and trading expeditions, the Palermo Stone mentions either the birth of two royal children or the creation of images of these children. One entry also records the foundation of thirty-five populated estates and twenty-two farms. The goods produced

and livestock raised on these estates and farms would have been dedicated to the royal house, both for the supply and sustenance of the living king and his retinue and also for the royal cult centered around the
king's mortuary complexes. In the fifteenth year of his reign, two important buildings, named "Sneferu high of the white crown" (the crown of
Upper Egypt) and "Sneferu high of the red crown" (the crown of Lower
Egypt) were erected; these were probably sacred in nature. Additional
events deemed worthy of recording for posterity were the visits of the
king to important national shrines and the fashioning of important statues, again of the king, in precious materials such as copper and gold.

Chapter Two

Sneferu at Meidum

Sneferu sat with his brother Neferma'at in the new palace at Meidum. They were
planning a new pyramid, the largest ever built, to tower to the sky. It would be a
step pyramid, such as kings had been building since the time of their great-great-
grandfather Djoser. The freshly painted throne room in which the two men met
glowed with color, scenes of the king defeating his enemies dominating the walls.
The wealth that was already pouring into the royal coffers from trade and military
expeditions would enable the king to build a fantastic monument, bigger and better
than any that had been built by his illustrious ancestors. The young king was full
of energy and ideas, arguing with his brother, who was also his vizier and chief
architect, about details of engineering, drawing plans on the papyrus he held across
his lap.

Aside from the events recorded on the Palermo Stone, much of what
we know about Sneferu's reign comes from the four pyramids that he
left behind. The mass of stone quarried and moved to build these pyra-

mids, leaving aside the goods and labor needed for their associated complexes, bears testimony to the enormous assets in both materials and manpower that Sneferu commanded. We can also catch a glimpse of the enormous wealth of the country through the funerary equipment of his queen, Hetepheres, found at the bottom of a shaft at Giza near the pyramid of her son Khufu. This rich burial included beautifully decorated objects of gilded wood and jewelry, including twenty exquisite silver bracelets inlaid with lapis lazuli, carnelian, and turquoise.

We do not know where Huni's court was located, but Sneferu set up his first capital at the site of Meidum, in the southernmost part of the Memphite region, overlooking the Faiyum Oasis. The kings of the 1st Dynasty had established a capital city near the apex of the Delta called Ineb-hedj ("white wall"), at the foot of the Saqqara plateau; and the monarchs of the Old Kingdom stayed in the Memphite region, bringing their courts with them to the sites of their pyramids so that they could keep an eye on the most important building projects of their reigns. This entire area was strategically important, as it was located near the point where the Nile Valley (Upper Egypt) met the Delta (Lower Egypt), and it also commanded the trade routes to the northeast.

Sneferu's administration consisted primarily of the members of his immediate family, who served as his advisers and made sure that his orders were carried out. The highest official in his court was the vizier. This title is attested only once before the time of Sneferu, associated with a late 2nd Dynasty official named Menka. Beginning in Sneferu's reign, an unbroken line of viziers stretches through the Old Kingdom. The vizier was second only to the king and was ultimately responsible for making sure the wishes of his monarch were fulfilled.

Sneferu's first attested vizier was a prince named Neferma'at. The mastaba tomb of this prince, which he shared with his wife, Atet, is located at Meidum. We know that he was an "eldest son of the king," but we do not know for certain which king was his father. He may have been the son of Huni and a minor queen and thus the half brother of

Sneferu. Alternatively, he might have been the eldest son of Sneferu himself, perhaps with a minor queen. As vizier, Neferma'at would have been directly responsible for many of the impressive achievements of Sneferu's reign. His title of overseer of all the king's works, i.e., chief architect, tells us that he was in charge of building, among other things, the royal tomb; thus he, or someone under him, must have been a brilliant engineer.

In order to understand the significance of the architectural developments that took place during the reign of Sneferu, it is useful to go back in time and trace the antecedents of the pyramidal tomb. The earliest kings of Egypt (Dynasties 0 and 1, c. 3150 to 2850 B.C.) were buried in progressively more elaborate tombs in the desert at Abydos in Middle Egypt (the site later sacred to the god Osiris). The tombs are in an area known as the Umm el Qa'ab ("mother of pots"); large funerary enclosures where the royal mortuary cult was carried out lie closer to the floodplain. In the 1st Dynasty, both the tombs and their "valley" enclosures were surrounded with rows of subsidiary graves containing the bodies of members of the royal household, sacrificed at the death of the king so that they could serve him in the afterlife.

There are also a number of extremely large and elaborate 1st Dynasty tombs in the form of mastabas (tombs with a low, rectangular superstructure named after the Arabic word for bench) at Saqqara, near the capital of Ineb-hedj. When these were first found, the excavator believed that *these* were the tombs of the 1st Dynasty kings, but many scholars now think that they belonged to high courtiers instead. However, given their location near the capital, enormous size, and elaborate architecture (combined with the fact that some of these, like the tombs at Abydos, are surrounded by subsidiary burials for sacrificed retainers), it is possible that at least some of these were cenotaphs for the kings themselves, additional foci for their cults, or were the tombs of queens or princes. In any event, several of the 2nd Dynasty kings were buried at Saqqara (in an area now under the upper temple of Unas, a king of the 5th Dynasty), although the last two have tombs and valley enclosures at Abydos (without associated human sacrifice, which had died out by the beginning of the 2nd Dynasty).

A number of these Early Dynastic tombs have a large mound built over the shaft leading to the burial chamber. In one case, the mound is in the form of a series of shallow steps. These mounds have a very clear significance: they represent the primeval mound on which the creator god stood to bring the universe into being.

The regularity of the agricultural cycle—the dryness of summer, the inundation followed by the reemergence and renewed fertility of the earth—so impressed the Egyptians that most of the different creation myths that have come down to us incorporate the image of a primeval mound arising out of the waters of chaos that existed before time, a mythological echo of the islands of earth that appeared each year at the recession of the flood. Three distinct versions are recorded, each from a different cult city. In the myth from the ancient city of On, or Iunu, now known as Heliopolis, a creator god, Atum, arose from the primeval mound and created two beings, Shu and Tefnut, who in turn created the sky goddess Nut and the earth god Geb. Geb and Nut's four children were Osiris, Isis, Nephthys, and Seth. Another version that includes this mound, from the Memphite theology, is more abstract: Ptah, the god of Memphis, arose from the primeval mound and gave the universe form through speech. It was also possible for the creation to be expressed through the feminine principle; like Atum and Ptah, the goddess Neith of Sais brought the world into being without a partner, conceiving all of the deities and human beings in her heart.

The first king of the 3rd Dynasty, Djoser, took this mound and transformed it into a huge stepped pyramid that towered to the sky. (Note that the word *pyramid* is a Greek term meaning "little cakes"; the Egyptians themselves used a different term, *mer*, for these monuments.) Although the Palermo Stone mentions a temple of stone built at the end of the 2nd Dynasty, there is evidence that this was never completed, so

Djoser's complex has taken official pride of place as the first monumental stone building ever constructed.

The step pyramid underwent a number of changes in plan. In the beginning, it was a single mastaba; the architects continued to add to it until it was a massive six-stepped structure leading to the heavens. This architectural change also reflected a modification in meaning: in addition to its function as the primeval mound upon which the deceased king—as an incarnation of the creator god—could stand to do his work, the step pyramid formed a ladder to the sky, up which the soul of the king could ascend in order to join his divine companions, the imperishable stars.

The Step Pyramid of Djoser was surrounded by an elaborate complex of temples and shrines, many of them nonfunctional structures designed to imitate actual shrines that would have existed in the world of the living. A high percentage of these structures seem to focus on the Sed festival. This important royal event was celebrated first after thirty years of a king's rule, and then could be repeated at shorter intervals afterward. The principal images of this festival show the king in a short, tight cloak or robe, seated on a throne, or in a short kilt and bare chest, holding a flail (perhaps a fly whisk, and certainly an important royal symbol) and running. The Sed festival is generally interpreted as a sort of jubilee at which the king's power was renewed and his strength ceremonially rejuvenated. It may also have celebrated the king's successful accomplishment of all that the gods had asked him to do, and thus marked the completion of his mortuary complex. Djoser's entire complex was surrounded by a huge wall decorated with niched panels in the style known as "palace facade," already seen around the Early Dynastic funerary enclosures at Abydos and the mastaba tombs at Saqqara. This type of paneling is thought, as the name suggests, to imitate the walls of the royal residence. The palace itself would have been built primarily of mud brick and decorated with reed matting.

Several of Djoser's 3rd Dynasty successors are known to have started step pyramid complexes, but none seems to have lived long enough to complete his tomb, and little can be successfully gleaned about the development of the royal tomb from this period. The burial place of the last king of this dynasty, Huni, has never been satisfactorily identified. There are, however, seven small pyramids located in Upper Egypt in a line along the west bank of the Nile stretching from Seila in the north to Elephantine in the south. These vary in their details but are similar in size and basic construction. All are step pyramids, and none possesses any interior chambers or attached structures, such as cult temples. Near the Elephantine pyramid, a granite cone was found which bore the name of Huni. It has been suggested that six of these seven pyramids (leaving aside, for now, the northernmost, at Seila) were built by Huni.

Some scholars have suggested that these step pyramids were symbols of the nomes, the administrative units into which Egypt was divided, and/or markers of provincial capitals where the king's representatives held sway; others think they might be tombs for queens who had been born in the provinces or sacred tombs associated with the myth of Horus and Seth. I believe that they were representations of the primeval mound associated with royal residences up and down the Nile. In any event, they may belong to Huni and, if so, are all we have for him in terms of pyramids.

The pyramid at Seila was built by Sneferu himself, the first of his four pyramids. It now stands at a height of seven meters (twenty-three feet), built of small chunks of limestone mixed with sand and mud. From a distance, it looks like a large mastaba, but closer inspection shows clearly that it was once a pyramid, built in steps. The base—of which only one side can be measured, at twenty-five meters (eighty-two feet) in length—is oriented slightly west of due north. On the blocks of this pyramid were found graffiti—a technical archaeological term for mason's marks and the like. There is no burial chamber in the Seila pyramid nor any evidence of a funerary temple, save faint traces of a mud-brick causeway on the east. Ludwig Borchardt, a German archaeologist active in the late nineteenth and early twentieth centuries, found a basalt fragment at the edge of the floodplain nearby, which might suggest that there were statues or a valley temple in this area.

It was originally thought that this pyramid belonged to the 3rd Dynasty, although no convincing evidence for this theory was ever put forth. Recent excavations in the area uncovered one complete and one fragmentary stele nearby. The first stele bore the name of Sneferu inside a *serekh*—a rectangle bordered on the bottom by a palace facade. This is topped by a representation of the god Horus. Similar steles bearing *serekhs* containing kings' names have been found identifying the royal owners of the Early Dynastic royal tombs, and this discovery shows clearly that the Seila pyramid belonged to Sneferu. Like the other small provincial pyramids, this may have served as a cult place representing the primeval mound associated with a royal palace.

Whatever the actual function of the Seila pyramid, Sneferu's first planned mortuary complex was at Meidum, in the western desert about a hundred kilometers (sixty-two miles) south of Cairo. Today, the pyramid there has the appearance of a tower built on top of a mound, the result of later quarrying activities that stripped its casing stones and led to its partial collapse. This pyramid has been explored by a number of adventurers and scholars; the first scientific excavations were carried out by an English scholar named John Perring in 1837.

It was once thought that this pyramid belonged to Sneferu's father, Huni, but this was primarily because no other tomb had been found for him. In fact, all the evidence points to Sneferu as the sole builder and cult recipient: later graffiti ascribes the pyramid to Sneferu, and Djed-Sneferu, the ancient name of the town of Meidum, supports this attribution.

Sneferu's Meidum pyramid followed the example set by his predecessors and was built as a series of stacked mastabas. It was begun as a seven-step pyramid, but, about the time the builders reached the fourth or fifth step, the plan was changed to accommodate an extra step. Its square base measured 144 meters (472 feet) on a side. The pyramid originally reached a height of 92 meters (302 feet).

The entrance to the interior chambers of the pyramid is located in the north face, about 30 meters (98 feet) from the ground. The entrance leads to a passageway, about 58 meters (187 feet) long, which slopes down to the bedrock at the base of the pyramid. The passageway runs horizontally for several meters, then a short vertical shaft leads straight up to the burial chamber, which lies within the body of the pyramid. The roof of this chamber was vaulted with what was then a novel technique, corbeling, in which the upper parts of the side walls were formed by overhanging each successive course of stone until they were close enough to cover with a single course of blocks. No trace of a burial was found within the chamber, but pieces of a wooden coffin, dated stylistically to this period, were found at the bottom of the vertical shaft.

In contrast to the pyramid complexes of the 3rd Dynasty, where the pyramid stands in the center, surrounded by various cult buildings and sacred spaces, the Meidum pyramid is the ultimate focus of a linear progression of other structures. It is the first complex laid out in this new design, which would remain the basic style of pyramid complexes for the rest of the Old Kingdom. The entrance to the complex would probably have been in a temple (called in other complexes a "valley temple") close to the edge of the floodplain or at least a landing platform, although no traces of this remain. From this area, a causeway leads to a small chapel against the eastern face of the pyramid. There were two round-topped steles in this chapel, but they had never been inscribed with the royal name. The pyramid and the small funerary chapel are surrounded by an enclosure wall.

Also within this enclosure wall, to the south of the main pyramid, is a smaller pyramid and a second tomb in the form of a mastaba. The small pyramid has been identified as Sneferu's cult, or satellite, pyramid. This feature became standard in later pyramid complexes, and theories about its function abound. Scholars trace this ritual structure back to Djoser's complex, which contained an enigmatic mastaba-like tomb to the south of the main pyramid. Beneath this tomb, known as the south tomb, were corridors similar to those under the main pyramid and decorated, like the main corridors, with niches filled with reliefs depicting Djoser performing rituals connected with his Sed festival. The "burial" chamber under the south tomb, in contrast to the main burial chamber, is square and too small to hold a sarcophagus.

Some scholars believe that the south tomb, and the later satellite pyramids, held the canopic jars containing the viscera of the king (although, as we will see later, the first evidence of canopic jars dates from the reign of either Sneferu or Khufu and many later complexes have emplacements for canopic chests in the main pyramid). Others theorize that it was a symbolic tomb for the king of Upper Egypt, the burial place of the royal crowns or the royal placenta, or the tomb of the royal *ka* (the life force of the king, the aspect of the soul that received the cult offerings). Other scholars think that these tombs were associated with the Sed festival. My personal theory is that, during the celebration of the Sed festival, the king took off his robe and crown and put on the kilt that he wore to perform the ritual run inside the cult pyramid.

A small mastaba lies north of the main pyramid, within the enclosure wall. Its burial chamber is small, but the passage leading to this chamber is impressive, lined with great beams and blocks of fine limestone. The chamber itself is roofed with a four-meter (fourteen-foot) beam of limestone—quite an impressive feat of engineering! A coffin was found in the northwest corner of the chamber, containing a skeleton with flexed knees lying with its head to the north and its face to the east. Pottery included with the burial dates it to the early 4th Dynasty, but no other information is available about the tomb's occupant. It is tempting to suppose that the skeleton is that of a queen, perhaps even of Sneferu's mother, Mersyankh, who was included in the later cult at Meidum. A much later graffito in the complex, dating from the New Kingdom (about one thousand years later), prays for the *ka*s of both Sneferu and Queen Mersyankh, so it is probable that this queen was buried at Meidum, and this mastaba would have been her most likely tomb. But without inscriptions, the owner of this tomb must officially remain a mystery.

A very large mastaba, numbered 17, lies at the northeast corner of Sneferu's enclosure wall. In it was a red granite sarcophagus, the oldest known of its type, containing a body that had been completely stripped of flesh; each bone was wrapped separately, then put in its original place and the body wrapped as a whole. No inscriptions have survived to identify the tomb owner. However, from the size and location of the mastaba, and the fact that it is the first private tomb built of stone, it is clear that it was built for an important prince. It is generally assumed that this was a son of Huni's, but it is equally, if not more likely, that this prince was Sneferu's son and that he died during the early part of his father's reign. Yet another theory is that this is actually the body of Huni himself.

Work must have gone on at Meidum for about fourteen years. A number of important nobles were buried at the site, indicating that it was the center of power for a significant period. Chief among these nobles was Sneferu's vizier Neferma'at and his wife, Atet. Their tomb was beautifully decorated with scenes depicting the family receiving offerings and servants performing the tasks of daily life. These scenes served to guarantee symbolically that the deceased were provided with the food they needed in their afterlife. They also had religious meaning and magically helped to ensure the proper functioning of the Egyptian universe.

The decoration in Neferma'at and Atet's tomb is particularly interesting because it illustrates the sort of experimentation that was a hallmark of Sneferu's reign. Some of the scenes in it were painted on plaster, but in others, the images and hieroglyphs were cut out and then filled with colored paste. This new technique was not terribly successful and was immediately abandoned. The burial chamber, which also contained a defleshed skeleton, had been plundered, probably soon after or even while it was being closed and blocked. This can be seen as evidence that the royal court had already moved on, so that security at the site was no longer tight. For elaborate as the complex at Meidum was, it was only the first of Sneferu's three major pyramid complexes, and the court would soon move on.

Chapter Three

Dahshur

Sneferu and the Cult of the Sun

The death of his favorite son left Sneferu feeling sad and weary. His crown prince was gone, never to take on the mantle of Horus on earth, never to rule the Two Lands, never to say the prayers and make the offerings at his father's tomb. Sneferu had built an enormous tomb for him, near the corner of his own pyramid at Meidum, and buried him in great style, but now he couldn't bear to be near it. Turning to action, always his answer to problems, he called in his vizier Neferma'at, and announced that they would abandon Meidum and move to a new site. The two men became absorbed in discussions of religion, poring over the old texts and striving to understand the will of the gods and the ways of ma'at. It would no longer be enough for the king to mount his eternal staircase and join the gods in the sky; he would become one with the sun god himself, Re, and be buried within the slanting rays of the sun.

In about the fifteenth year of his reign, Sneferu decided to build a new type of pyramid, and he abandoned his complex at Meidum, leaving behind his capital city in favor of the more northerly site of Dahshur. It is hard to know exactly why he made this move. Was Dahshur a more strategic location, giving him better control over the Delta and a more convenient place from which to launch military campaigns? But Meidum and Dahshur are not far from each other—both are in the Memphite region—so it is hard to imagine that such a small move would make such a huge tactical difference. Dahshur is certainly closer to the Early Dynastic capital of the country and the northern cult places of Sneferu's ancestors at Saqqara, so this may have been a contributing factor. Was the change due to a family problem? Had Sneferu's crown prince died? It is possible that the skeleton found in tomb 17 at Meidum was a son of Sneferu's. But it may be that none of these reasons alone is sufficient explanation for such a move.

At the time, Dahshur was a virgin site and seemed an excellent location for the monumental display of status that Sneferu and his architects and advisers had planned. I believe that the decision to move was most likely prompted in the main by a shift in religious dogma, for this is the moment at which the concept of the true pyramid, with its blatantly solar overtones, came into being.

Let me take a moment now to talk about how we, as scholars, try to reconstruct the ancient meanings of the structures we excavate. The architecture of the monuments themselves can tell us a great deal, and we can supplement this data with the many images and texts that the ancient Egyptians left behind. Often, we must look to later sources for information about earlier structures and try to extrapolate backward. For the Old Kingdom, we are fortunate to have a very important series of texts, known as the Pyramid Texts, at our disposal. These texts have been found inscribed in the interior chambers of pyramids from the late 5th and 6th Dynasties, and consist of a series of spells designed to aid the king in his transition to the afterlife. They were composed in order to explain the relationship of the king to the gods, ensure the king's proper transition to a state of divinity, and help him travel to meet the sun god. The archaic language used in these spells tells us that they must have been written earlier than the late 5th Dynasty; it is possible that before this time, they were set down on more perishable materials. However, archaeological and architectural evidence must always take precedence over supposition when analyzing ancient Egyptian monuments.

The true pyramid, while retaining its meaning as primeval mound and stairway to the stars, also represents the rays of the sun as they stream down to earth. It echoes the form of the *benben*, a pointed stone that was the solar symbol par excellence, thought to have existed in reality as an object, perhaps a stone with a rounded top or an ancient meteorite. This artifact was kept in the main temple at On, northeast of modern Cairo, which is known to us by its Greek name of Heliopolis ("city of the sun") and was the center of solar worship in pharaonic Egypt from at least the Old Kingdom on.

According to mythology that has been reconstructed from various sources, including the Pyramid Texts, the sun god Re was the ruler of the gods. His daughter was Hathor, also important to the royal house as the wife of Horus, whom each king in turn embodied. As we have seen, Horus, in addition to his role as son of Osiris, was also known as the son of Re (and, in the somtimes contradictory belief system of the Egyptians, also the son of Hathor). The priests at On linked Re with the ancient god of their city, Atum, and he became known as Atum-Re. Atum was the creator god, inherent in the unformed cosmos, and when he emerged on the primeval mound to create the world he took the form of a newborn child, Nefertem/Re, the god of the sun. Scenes of this legend, all from much later in Egyptian history, depict a large lotus flower coming into view as the primeval waters of the chaos that preceded the creation parted. Inside the lotus sits the sun god as a child, finger in his mouth in the gesture of youth. Another type of scene shows the newborn child emerging from the primeval mound on the back of a cow in the midst of endless water.

In yet another version of this tale, the *benben* arose from the vast waters. The sun god, in the shape of a phoenix (the benu bird), stood on this stone. Inscriptions from later in the Old Kingdom refer to the capstones of pyramids as "*benbenet*," a clear reference to the *benben* stone. Thus, with each sunset, Re died as he slipped below the western horizon, and spent the night battling with the demons and dangers of the netherworld in order to join the god Osiris and be born anew at dawn, reiterating daily the moment of creation.

The name of one king of the 2nd Dynasty, Raneb ("Re/the sun is lord"), suggests that the sun god was worshipped by this time (around 2850 B.C.). We know that the cult of Re was important from at least the time of Djoser in the 3rd Dynasty. Relief fragments from a shrine depicting this king and three royal women (probably his mother, his principal queen, and his eldest daughter) have been found at On. One of Djoser's names, seen on the base of a famous statue of the king in his Sed festival robe, which was found in a *serdab* (enclosed statue chamber) near his mortuary temple, was Ra-nebu ("Re of gold"). We also know that the sun god was worshipped in a special temple called *per-nebu* ("house of gold") at On; gold was the material of the sun—shining, yellow, and impervious to rust and decay.

In the reign of Huni, an important solar symbol appeared for the first time. This is the cartouche, an oval enclosing the royal name. We know from later texts that this represented "all that the sun disk encircles," and clearly associated the king with the sun god. Another way we can see that the solar cult was gaining in importance during the early 4th Dynasty is that a number of Sneferu's highest officials held the title of "greatest seer of On" (high priest of Heliopolis). These men would have served as the chief astronomers responsible for tracking the sun and stars.

It is possible that the priesthood of Re at On had grown in power over the course of the 3rd Dynasty, and perhaps even threatened the power of the king. Sneferu, rather than following the traditional royal dogma—in which the king was Horus on earth and became the sun god at death—may have announced that he was Re both in life and after death. The evidence for this is the new shape in which he built his pyramid and the fact that he chose to place his burial chamber within the mass of the superstructure rather than underneath.

It is generally held that Sneferu planned to build one pyramid at Dahshur, at the south end of the site. According to the standard reconstruction of events, Sneferu planned this pyramid, which he called the "shining pyramid" (another solar allusion), very carefully. The original slope was 60 degrees, a fairly steep incline. Work went along smoothly for a while, until the monument had reached a height of about 40 meters (131 feet), and then cracking suddenly developed in the outer casing and in the interior passageways. It seems that the rock on which the foundations had been laid was unstable and the angle of the outer faces was too steep. The solution was to change the design, and the engineers built a girdle at a slope of 54 degrees around the lower part of the pyramid, then reduced the slope of the upper part to 43 degrees before Sneferu finally abandoned the project and started a new pyramid to the north. The pyramid in consequence has an odd profile, and has been nicknamed the Bent Pyramid by Egyptologists. The base is 188 meters (617 feet) square, and its height is 105 meters (345 feet).

A great deal of progress had been made on both the pyramid and its complex before it was supposedly abandoned, and much of the site has been carefully excavated. Like the Meidum complex, the Bent Pyramid complex was entered at the east, near the edge of the cultivation, through a valley temple. This was excavated in the 1950s by the great Egyptian Egyptologist Ahmed Fakhry. When he arrived at the site, all that pointed to the existence of this structure was a large area covered with limestone chips. Fakhry assumed that whatever had once stood there had been mostly carried away by people taking the stones to build with, and he hoped at the most to be able to distinguish its plan. On the very first day of excavations, after only an hour and twenty minutes of work, his team uncovered a high limestone wall, part

of the lost valley temple. Soon afterward, they began to discover fragments of reliefs and statues.

The walls of this temple were covered with beautiful reliefs that had
been carved in fine limestone and painted in vibrant colors. We believe
that the valley temple was the place at which materials from the outside
were brought into the sacred space of the pyramid complex and dedicated to the use of the king, the point of transition between the secular
and the sacred. Some of the valley temple reliefs immortalize this function by representing female personifications of Sneferu's provincial estates (such as the ones mentioned on the Palermo Stone) carrying
provisions for the royal cult.

These processions of offering bearers give us important information
about the vast extent of the lands held by the royal house. Some figures
are from Upper Egypt, and some from Lower Egypt, so the royal hold-
ings clearly stretched the length of the Nile. The majority of the regions
that can be identified lay in the area of Middle Egypt, where the floodplain was wide, but it is likely that there were many estates in the fertile
Delta whose names have not survived.

Other reliefs from this temple are equally fascinating. Several show
the king performing rites from the Sed festival (sitting on the throne
wearing the double crown and his Sed festival robe, and wearing a kilt
and performing the Sed festival run); others show him visiting the temple of Buto (an important early shrine), founding a temple, giving offerings to the gods, and even embracing several gods. Fragments from three
statues were also found inside the temple (and it is thought that there
were originally six). Enough of one of these was recovered to enable its
recent restoration by the German Institute in Cairo. It depicts the king
with the white crown of Upper Egypt on his head, wearing a linen skirt,
and is now on display at the Cairo Museum.

From the valley temple enclosure, a causeway leads to the northeast-
ern corner of the wall that surrounds the pyramid. Set against the east
face of the pyramid is a small open-air chapel containing an alabaster of-

fering table. Flanking the chapel were two round-topped steles bearing an image of the king in his Sed festival robe and the double crown along with his titulary (his names and titles) within a *serekh*.

To the south of the main pyramid is a smaller pyramid, once thought to belong to Hetepheres, Sneferu's main queen. However, this structure has now been definitely identified as Sneferu's cult pyramid, which would have served the same purpose as the one at Meidum. The interior chambers are an abbreviated version of the chambers in the main pyramid but, as in Djoser's complex, the burial chamber is not large enough to hold a sarcophagus. Against the east face of this small pyramid is an offering place in which were found two more round-topped steles bearing the names of Sneferu.

The interior chambers of the Bent Pyramid can be entered either from the north or west. From the northern entrance, high up on the pyramid's north face, a long passageway slopes down to the bedrock. Here, an antechamber was built and roofed with a corbeled vault. Above this is the burial chamber, which must have been reached by stairs or a ladder. It also has a corbeled roof. The entrance in the western face of the pyramid slopes down to a point above the bedrock before leveling into a passage leading to a second corbeled burial chamber. At some point, someone who knew exactly where both burial chambers were hacked out a rough passage between them.

A very strange discovery was made by English archaeologists John Perring and Richard Howard Vyse as they explored this pyramid in the late 1830s. Their workmen were clearing the interior passages and suffering greatly from the intense heat. On October 15, 1839, they opened a tunnel that led to one of the interior chambers. Suddenly, they were greeted by a refreshing draft of cool air, so strong that it blew out their torches. The wind continued for two days, and then stopped as suddenly as it had started, leaving the archaeologists completely mystified as to its source. The only reasonable explanation is that there is a connection between this room and the outside of the pyramid; we know that it could not have come through the western tunnel, as this wasn't opened until 1951 by Ahmed Fakhry.

Fakhry, in the course of his work at Dahshur, made another strange discovery: sometimes, as the wind blew in from the desert, it made an eerie wailing that could be heard inside the pyramid, especially from the upper end of the western passage. This noise would continue for about ten seconds and then stop. The only explanation Fakhry found satisfying was that some parts of the pyramid interior have not yet been discovered, and that these parts connect with the outside.

I recently took twelve of my students from the American University in Cairo to explore the interior chambers of this unique pyramid. We climbed up to the northern entrance, then entered a tunnel 80 meters (263 feet) long and only 1.10 meters (3.6 feet) high. We had to hunch to make our way to the first corbeled chamber. From there, we had to climb 6.25 meters (20.5 feet) up some rather rickety wooden stairs to reach the floor of the lower burial chamber. Inside, we found two tunnels leading from the south wall to a shaft, but they did not seem to continue. We saw another tunnel, about 12 meters long (39 feet), leading from the floor to another tunnel that was oriented east-west. We headed west, and found the second burial chamber. We could see the cedar beams that Sneferu's expedition to ancient Byblos had brought back millennia before, still in good shape. We could also feel cold air coming from the exterior of the pyramid via some indeterminate source—one clue that this pyramid still holds mysteries to be solved.

The fact is that, whatever engineering problems may have occurred, the Bent Pyramid and its complex were completed and cased with fine, expensive white limestone. For this reason, I have my doubts that the generally accepted explanation is the correct one. I believe it possible that both the Bent Pyramid and its companion, the Red Pyramid, were planned from the beginning of the move to Dahshur. Perhaps Sneferu always meant to be buried in the Bent Pyramid and had the second pyramid at Dahshur built as a sort of red herring; or perhaps the entire layout of the site, with two pyramids, had some cultic significance.

Whatever the reasons and the exact sequence of events, in the twenty-ninth year of his reign, Sneferu found another suitable area a short distance to the north of the Bent Pyramid and started a fourth pyramid, a straight-sided one with a slope of 43 degrees. It was planned as the biggest pyramid yet, with a base length of 220 meters (722 feet) and a finished height of 105 meters (345 feet). He called this one, like the last, "the Shining Pyramid." Egyptologists have nicknamed it the Red Pyramid, because the stone that Sneferu used to build it has a reddish hue. By this time, the mechanics of pyramid building were much better understood, and work on the new monument went smoothly.

A German Egyptologist named Rainer Stadelmann has been working at this pyramid for many years and has made some remarkable discoveries. In the debris that lies around the base of the pyramid, he has found a number of pieces of the original limestone casing that bear graffiti left by the work gangs who built the pyramid. These are invaluable, as they often give regnal dates, and thus allow us to reconstruct the amount of time it took to build the pyramid; they also give us important information about the length of Sneferu's reign.

The highest date that Stadelmann has found is Count 24, which is equivalent to the forty-fifth or forty-sixth year of Sneferu's reign. The ancient Egyptian government took a census of cattle every two years, and kings of the early periods numbered their reigns according to these censuses. However, we know that there were several annual censuses during Sneferu's reign, so we cannot simply multiply the count by two. Stadelmann has also found pieces of the original capstone of the pyramid. This was a piece of fine limestone, uninscribed. In later periods, capstones were more elaborate affairs, and could be made of special stone, cased with costly materials such as electrum and/or inscribed.

There are some remains of a valley temple associated with this pyramid, but they have never been properly excavated; there are also possible traces of an unfinished causeway linking this temple with the main pyramid. The mortuary temple against the east face of the pyramid is significantly larger than the chapels at Meidum and the Bent Pyramid, but it seems to have been finished in a hurry, perhaps at the death of the king.

The entrance to the interior chambers of the pyramid opens from the center of the north face. A long passage leads to ground level, then a short horizontal passage leads to the first of two large corbeled antechambers. From the second antechamber, a horizontal passage high up in the southern wall leads to the burial chamber, which was constructed within the pyramid core. As in the Bent Pyramid, the location of the burial chamber above the level of the ground may have served symbolically to associate Sneferu with the sun god Re, rising within his horizon. This becomes more explicit in the pyramid of his son Khufu, whose pyramid complex is called Akhet Khufu ("horizon of Khufu").

At some point during the construction of the Red Pyramid, Sneferu sent a team back to Meidum to change his monument there from a step pyramid to a true pyramid by filling in the steps with a smooth-sided casing. The Meidum pyramid thus brought his building projects full cycle and represents both the beginning and the end of his reign. By this point, Sneferu had built more, in terms of sheer mass of stone moved, than any king before him, and his record remained unbroken (although it was challenged by the work of his son Khufu) to the end of the Old Kingdom.

Chapter Four

The Court of Sneferu

*Sneferu delighted in the antics of his young son, Khufu. The boy was only five, but
already had a mind of his own. His high, piping voice sent his nurses scrambling,
trying to avert a tantrum that might offend the ears of the king; but his doting
father simply laughed, thanking the gods for sending him this priceless gift, a son to
come after him on the Great Throne. He had thought his queen Hetepheres too old
to bear another child after the death of their first son, but she had done marvelously
well and was as gentle and beautiful as ever. And the boy was a wonder—strong,
quick, demanding, but also capable of sitting quietly for hours, listening to music or
drawing. He was already beginning to show interest in studying, a necessity for a
royal prince. Yes, his boy would be a great king someday, and would see to his cult
after his own death.*

Sneferu and his court lived near the sites of his pyramids, at first in
Meidum and later in Dahshur. The country was controlled from the
centrally located palace, the point where Upper and Lower Egypt were

unified. We can imagine Sneferu meeting with his vizier Neferma'at in order to receive information on the wealth of the land and the well-being of his subjects, news of his foreign campaigns and trade expeditions, and reports on the progress of his pyramid complexes.

So far, only the foundations of Old Kingdom palaces have been found, but fragments from New Kingdom palaces suggest that the walls were decorated with beautiful paintings, perhaps of the king smiting his enemies, of craftsmen building enormous wooden ships and the royal fleet sailing to foreign cities such as Byblos, and of the king making offerings to the gods of Egypt. The colors would have been bright and clear and in the best of the new court style, preserved for us on the walls of the tombs of Sneferu's nobles.

The tomb scenes also give us information about life in ancient Egypt. They depict many different activities: carpenters building boats; agricultural workers tending the fields; fishermen pulling in their nets; and offering bearers carrying birds or animals, heaping platters of food, and jars of wine, to name only a few. Scenes found for the first time in the tombs of Sneferu's nobles, and echoing scenes from his mortuary complexes, show personified nomes or estates carrying the products of their home territories to offer in the cults.

It is these tombs that give us the most information about Sneferu's family and officials. We know some of their names and, through their titles, can glean some ideas about what they did. Our reconstruction is necessarily fragmentary: we are dealing with accidents of preservation and discovery, and the information itself can be ambiguous. For example, Sneferu's first vizier, Neferma'at, is a "king's son." However, our translation of "son" is not completely accurate: during this period, the term was also used for a royal grandson. In any event, the name of Neferma'at's father is never given, so we must decide whether he was Huni's son or Sneferu's based on the dating of his tomb and what we can guess about his age relative to Sneferu's. Neferma'at and his wife, Atet, had a son named Hemiunu, who seems to have been a contemporary of Khufu's and served as vizier for much of his reign. Thus it is possible, as suggested above, that Neferma'at was Sneferu's brother or cousin, rather than his son.

However, given the length of the reigns of both Sneferu and Khufu, it is likely that Khufu was born later in his father's lifetime, so Neferma'at could have been a much older brother. This brings us to one of the difficult questions that have yet to be answered satisfactorily by Egyptologists: how was the succession determined? If Neferma'at was an older brother of Khufu's, then one might think he should have become king instead. Most Egyptologists assume that Old Kingdom rulers could have more than one wife at a time (as was certainly the case in the New Kingdom) and that one woman bore the title of principal queen. The traditional assumption is that it was the eldest son of this queen who ascended to the throne, so the king might have an older son by a minor wife who would not stand in the direct line of succession. The truth is, we do not know the answers to many questions like these; we can only make a guess based on the most likely scenario.

We do know that many of the young men who grew up at Sneferu's court went on to serve his son, and several of Sneferu's princesses became queens of the new king.

Another important tomb at Meidum belongs to a king's son named Rahotep, whose principal titles were great seer of Heliopolis (chief priest of the sun cult) and overseer of the army (general). Rahotep and his wife, Nofret, were buried at Meidum, and two exquisite statues of vibrantly painted limestone were walled up in one of the chambers of their tomb. Rahotep seems to belong to the same generation as Neferma'at, so it is likely that he was a son of Huni but also possible that he was a son of Sneferu. Nofret was a king's acquaintance, a title held by many Egyptian noblemen and women.

Mastaba tombs and some fragmentary statues found at Dahshur, associated with both the southern and northern pyramids, tell us about more possible members of the royal family, although in general their exact relationships to Sneferu are unclear. A number of monuments belong to men who call themselves "king's son," or even "king's son of his body," but this is not much help. We must look at the date of the tomb as well to be able to guess how each individual might fit into the family. The most important son of Sneferu was, of course, Khufu, who succeeded him on the throne of Egypt. However, Khufu does not appear on any of his father's monuments, so our information about this remarkable king comes from monuments dating to his own reign and later.

Sneferu was remembered in later tradition as a modest man, fiercely intelligent and curious, willing to listen to others, loving pleasure, and generous to his subjects. We are fortunate to have two ancient texts that provide personal glimpses, albeit apocryphal, of this extraordinary king. Both stories are thought to have been composed in the Middle Kingdom, half a millennium after Sneferu's death. The first is known as the Prophecy of Neferti.

The tale begins with a group of high officials known as the "magistrates of the residence" coming to the palace to greet the king, perhaps to receive their orders for the day. After they all left, Sneferu turned to his seal bearer and asked him to go fetch them back. When they returned (crawling on their bellies to him as a sign of respect), the king asked them to find someone clever with words—a son, brother, friend—who could come and entertain him. The officials suggested a priest of Bastet named Neferti (also described as a native of the center of the sun cult, Heliopolis), and so Sneferu sent for him.

Neferti arrived at the palace and made his obeisance, whereupon Sneferu said to him: "Come, Neferti, my friend, speak to me some fine words, choice phrases at the hearing of which my majesty may be entertained!"* Neferti asked whether he would prefer to hear tales of the past

* Translation from Miriam Lichtheim, *Ancient Egyptian Literature*, p. 140.

or prophecies of the future. The king replied, "Of what will happen. As soon as today is here, it is passed over." And he then took up his scribal kit (a papyrus roll, an ink palette, and a brush) and wrote down Neferti's words with his own hand.

The story told by Neferti is not pertinent here—it was a prophecy about the future and was evidently composed to justify the reign of the first king of the 12th Dynasty, Amenemhet I. But the tale as a whole is very interesting and provides us with the image of an intelligent, literate king; a powerful monarch whose subjects approached him on their bellies; and a man of great energy who had time, in the midst of all his building projects and wars, to be bored!

The second Middle Kingdom story about Sneferu is one of a series of tales (unfortunately incomplete) featuring kings and princes of the 4th Dynasty found on a document called the Westcar Papyrus. The setting is the palace of Khufu, who is being entertained by the storytelling of his own sons. In the first of these tales preserved in its entirety, Prince Baufre tells of a wondrous event from the reign of Sneferu. One day, the king was sad and upset, and asked everyone around him to help him find a way to remove his sadness. No one could help, so he called for a man named Djadjaemankh, a scribe and chief lector priest (who read the ritual in the temple). When Djadjaemankh arrived, Sneferu, addressing him as "brother," said to him: "I brought all the people in the palace to find a way to make me happy, but no one could help me."

Djadjaemankh recommended that Sneferu go to the palace lake and take a boat ride, get some fresh air and sunshine, and enjoy the beautiful "fields and shores" of his domain. To add to his pleasure, the priest suggested that the boat be rowed by the most beautiful women of the palace. Sneferu latched onto the idea immediately, and said: "Indeed, I shall go boating! Let there be brought to me twenty oars of ebony plated with gold, their handles of sandalwood plated with electrum. Let there be brought to me twenty women with the shapeliest bodies, breasts, and braids, who have not yet given birth. Also let there be brought to me twenty nets and give these nets to these women in place of their clothes!"*

The boat ride was a great success, and Sneferu was enjoying himself immensely when the leader of the girls, who was busy playing with her hair, lost her new fish-shaped turquoise pendant. She stopped rowing and so did the rest of the women on her side of the boat. When the king asked what was wrong, the girl told him. So he said to her, "Row! I shall replace it for you!" But the girl insisted that she wanted that pendant, not another. So the king sent for Djadjaemankh, who uttered a magic spell and folded the water back on itself so that they could see the bottom. And there was the pendant, lying on a potsherd on the bottom of the lake. The girl retrieved her pendant, and the king spent the rest of the day enjoying himself in the palace, and rewarded the priest for his help.

The image conveyed by these stories is of a king modest enough to call a lector priest "brother" and sensitive enough to cater to the whim of a lady who was not even royal. He clearly loved fun and pleasure. Whether or not this is an accurate reflection of reality, it is how he was remembered and may well have had some basis in truth. Taken with all of his actual feats, he must certainly have been a man of great energy! It is no wonder that this king built four pyramids.

* Actually made of beads and often worn over a sheath dress; here they are to be worn without the dress underneath.

Chapter Five

The King Is Dead

The palace was hushed with grief. The breath had finally flown from the body of

the king, and now it was time to prepare for the funeral, so that the proper order of

things could be maintained and the soul of the king rejoined with his body. Khufu

and Neferma'at met in the chamber of death, and spoke the correct prayers over

the body. The next seventy days would be crucial to the successful journey of

the king into the realm of the gods. The body was taken away to the wabet, *the*

mortuary workshop, and the preparations were commenced to send the god to join

his brethren in the sky.

*S*neferu died sometime between the forty-sixth and fifty-fourth years
of his reign, before the Red Pyramid and its complex were complete. We
can reconstruct the sequence of events that would have taken place after his death from later scenes and texts. Once his body had been taken
to the mortuary workshop, known as the *wabet*, it was placed within the
per-nefer ("good house"), where it underwent the process of mummification. Techniques of preserving the body were still in their infancy, but

the scientists who served Sneferu had made great advances during his reign. They had recently discovered that removing the internal organs—specifically the lungs, liver, stomach, and intestines—helped with the preservation of the body, so these were removed through an incision in the royal abdomen, dried in a solution of natron (hydrous sodium carbonate), wrapped separately, and stored in one of the four compartments of a canopic box. The heart, as the seat of the intellect, was left within the chest cavity.

The brain was also dangerous to leave in place, as it would liquefy and decay rapidly. We know from later examples that it was removed via a hole pierced through the nasal cavity or the back of the skull. A purgative liquid may have been injected into the brain cavity and the resulting matter drained out through the same hole. These initial preparations probably took about four days, after which the body was packed in natron and completely desiccated, a procedure that took between thirty and forty days.

Then came the artwork. The embalmer's job was to turn the emaciated body into something resembling its former self. During the early experimental phase of mummification, this was done by wrapping many layers of linen bandages around the body, impregnating this linen with plaster, and shaping the resulting material into the form of the original body, complete with details such as toenails and warts. Special attention would have been paid to the face, which would have been molded to look as much as possible like the living king. When this process had been completed, Sneferu's mummy would have been moved from the *per-nefer* to the place of purification, so that the rituals of purification and fumigation with incense could be carried out properly. Then the body was prepared for its final journey to the tomb.

The funeral itself would most likely have been a magnificent event. There would have been musicians and dancers, and priests saying prayers over an enormous banquet of offerings. The procession to the king's final resting place might have included his chief queen, Hetepheres, and certainly his heir, Khufu. We can imagine (and see in later tomb scenes) women wailing, tearing their clothes and their hair, and sometimes collapsing from grief.

Many scholars believe that Sneferu was buried in the Red Pyramid, his last monument, and there were indeed bones found in the debris filling one of the chambers in the northern pyramid. Some of these were human and included parts of a skull with evidence of some sort of mummification in the form of wrappings of fine-quality linen that had been impregnated with a dark resinlike substance. All the human remains appear to belong to one male skeleton. He had been past middle age at the time of death, as demonstrated by the degree of wear on his teeth, but he wasn't terribly old. He was relatively small, and probably—according to Ahmed Batrawi, the scientist who first studied the bones—had a strong constitution. One of the most remarkable aspects of this skeleton was that two of the toes were actually dummies. There were also animal bones, from a bull or cow, a camel, a donkey, and a dog; and there was a horn and a hoof possibly from a sheep, containing a roll of coarse linen. These animal bones may have been part of the original burial. The camel bones are unusual but not unheard of: camel bones were also found in some Early Dynastic Period burials at Helwan. In any case, it is possible, but far from proven, that the skeleton here is that of Sneferu.

I do not believe these bones belong to Sneferu, because I think Sneferu was actually buried inside the Bent Pyramid, where his later cult was focused, and may still lie hidden within secret chambers that have never been explored. The relieving chamber, and the mysterious draft that blows into this chamber, hint at mysteries still to be solved. For such a secret to be kept, it would have necessarily been limited to a small number of conspirators: Khufu himself, certainly; Neferma'at; and perhaps the young princes Ankhhaf and Hemiunu, who later served Khufu as his viziers. The burial would be blocked by huge slabs of granite that no one could move, and the tomb robbers would mistakenly believe that the king lay inside his last monument, the Red Pyramid at Dahshur.

Khufu would have conducted the funeral rites himself, proclaiming his father to be Re and Osiris, and himself taking the role of Horus on earth. The queens would have played the parts of Hathor, daughter of Re and wife of Horus; and of Isis and Nephthys, sisters and chief mourners of Osiris. Once the Opening of the Mouth, a ritual that gave magical life to images of the king (including the mummy itself), had been performed, the offering cult would have been activated and would have been carried out continuously by the *hemu-netjer* ("servants of the god"), whose duties were to see to the needs of the deity, in this case Sneferu, and celebrate the rituals in the god's sanctuary, in this case the deified king's mortuary temple.

Sneferu's cult survived into the Middle Kingdom, seven centuries after his death, focused on his Bent Pyramid at Dahshur. In this valley temple were found statues of private people, steles, and altars. Alterations were made to the chapel against the east face of this pyramid by later priests, and a group of Middle Kingdom incense altars inscribed for Sneferu were found here, left by a family of priests who were all named after him. This chapel was modified as late as the Ptolemaic period, when it seems as though a small group of priests tried to revive the cult of the ancient king, dead by then for over two thousand years. Several 12th Dynasty kings built their pyramids at Dahshur, near Sneferu's monuments, and there are many tombs of the Old and Middle Kingdoms at the site. Many children's names of the Middle Kingdom were compounded with the name of Sneferu.

This king, along with Hathor and the god Soped, was considered the patron saint of the Sinai turquoise mines. Amenemhet III, sixth king of the 12th Dynasty, mentions Sneferu's name in an inscription he left in the Wadi Maghara. Sneferu's reputation as a good king survived into

the New Kingdom, when he was honored by one of the sons of Rameses II, and even into the time of the Greek historian Herodotus, who visited Egypt in the fifth century B.C. The innovations and advances of his
reign laid the foundation for the glory now to come, the golden rule of
his son, Khufu.

Part Two

The Reign
of the Sun God

Chapter Six

The Early Reign of Khufu

The funeral was over; the old king had been laid to rest in his pyramid, and the new king had been crowned. All was in order. It was time to start the cycle anew, to choose a site for the pyramid that would serve as the focus for the new king's cult. The new vizier, Hemiunu, who was succeeding his father, Neferma'at, met with the young king in his private chambers in the palace at Dahshur, away from the pomp and formality of the throne room where the old king had attended to public matters of state. The decision was up to the two most important men in the land. The royal scientists had surveyed the various possibilities and made their reports, and the king and his vizier had only to make the final choice. "It is a good site, your majesty," said Hemiunu. "The rock beneath the sand is good; we can quarry stones right near the pyramid itself and build a great benben to bear eternal witness to your power and greatness. The floodplain to the east is broad and fertile; the canal of Menes brings the waters of the river close to us, so it will be an ideal place for your palace and city." The young king agreed with his adviser, and the royal entourage prepared to travel to Giza to inspect the new site.

*I*n the first year of his reign, Sneferu's heir took the name Khnum-Khufwy, which means "it is the god Khnum who protects me." Khnum, whose animal totem was the ram, had two principal roles: he was the protector of the southern border of Egypt, with a cult center at Aswan, and he was a fertility god who fashioned human beings from mud, worshipped primarily in Middle Egypt, near modern Minya. There was a town near this cult center called Menat-Sneferu ("nurse of Sneferu"), which was later changed to Menat-Khufu ("nurse of Khufu"). This suggests that the royal family of the 4th Dynasty had some connection with this region of Egypt; it is likely that Khufu took this name to ensure the protection of this powerful god.

Shortly after taking the throne, Khufu added the Horus name Medjedu to his titulary. The translation of this name is "one who strikes or hits" and suggests that Khufu came to the throne planning to continue his father's military expeditions abroad. This name appears with the tutelary goddesses of Upper and Lower Egypt, Nekhbet and Wadjet, and with the epithets "king of Upper and Lower Egypt." Khnum-Khufwy was also known in his early years as Hor-neb-rekhu, which means "Horus, lord of knowledge," and may bear some connection to his later reputation as a scientist and man of great learning. Like his father, he had a golden Horus name, in his case written with two falcons above the sign for gold.

Khufu and Hemiunu had chosen well in selecting Giza as the site of the new capital. It lay in the western desert, already the traditional location for a royal tomb, with its links to the setting sun. The geology of the plateau was ideal for pyramid building, for it included an outcropping of a limestone formation (called by geologists the Mokattam formation) that would provide good material for the royal monuments. There are three strata running through the plateau: two layers are weak in one way or another, with cracks and hollows or easily weathered surfaces; but the third level has excellent-quality stone. All three strata would prove useful. This is also evidence that the ancient Egyptians understood geology and had studied the rock of the plateau carefully. Perhaps, as we have fantasized in our introduction, a group of ancient scientists had even visited various other sites in the region before they chose Giza.

A great canal ran south to north through the floodplain east of the plateau. Tradition held that this had been cut by Aha (Menes), first king of the 1st Dynasty; it is now known in Arabic as the Bahr Yousef (the sea of Joseph). Beginning to the south, it runs parallel to the Nile for a distance of about two hundred kilometers (124 miles) before turning west toward the Faiyum Oasis, then turning north again at the Sea of Libya to empty into the Mediterranean near Alexandria.

The first order of business to prepare for the move to Giza was to build a palace, administrative quarters, and houses for the court. It was here that the king, his family, and his nobles would have their primary residences. In the years between 1988 and 1994, in the course of preparing for and building a new sewage system (carefully supervised by the Egyptian Antiquities Department) under the modern suburb of Nazlet el-Samman, which presses against the foot of the plateau, some remarkable discoveries were made. At the western edge of the floodplain to the north end of the plateau were the foundations of a large limestone building that may be the remains of Khufu's palace. Stretching for several kilometers to the east and south, we caught glimpses of a settlement of mud-brick houses from the Old Kingdom, the remains of the capital city of Khufu and his heirs.

Once the living quarters had been built, plans for the pyramid and its complex could proceed. One of Hemiunu's titles, like that of his father, was overseer of all the king's work; thus we know that he was the chief architect, ultimately responsible for all aspects of the pyramid-building process. The northern end of the plateau was chosen as the site of the pyramid itself, leaving room to the south for the tombs of Khufu's successors.

It is easy to imagine Hemiunu and his staff drawing plans, either on papyrus or on large flakes of smooth limestone, to show to the king and guide them in their work. It is possible that scale models were also built—a model of the burial chambers of an unknown king who reigned about five hundred years later was found inside a 12th Dynasty pyramid temple at Dahshur. Perhaps there was even a building office at the foot of the plateau. We know for certain that the men (and we are quite sure that they were men) responsible for planning and building the complex were highly trained in the science of engineering, able to use astronomy, mathematics, and simple physics to put their ideas into practice.

The first step was to level the site and mark out the exact location of the pyramid. The ancient surveyors succeeded in orienting the pyramid base to the cardinal points to an astonishing degree of accuracy, within a fraction of 1 degree, a feat requiring highly developed astronomical skills. A number of scholars have made suggestions about the exact techniques that might have been used. For example, the ancient surveyors could have built a circular wall of mud brick, rising to the height of a man's eyes, and left it unroofed. One man would have stood in the center of this structure and, on the top of the wall, made perfectly level by the use of a channel of water, marked the rise and fall of a certain star as it passed the horizon at dusk and again at dawn. Using a plumb line (ancient Egyptian *merkhet*), these marks would be extended to ground level, then lines would have been drawn connecting these points with the center of the circle marked out by the wall. By bisecting the angle created between the two lines, the ancient Egyptians could have found true north.

Another possible method has been proposed recently by an English Egyptologist named Kate Spence, who was interested in explaining why Khufu's pyramid is so accurately aligned to true north, while the pyramids of his successors are less precisely laid out. We know that the ancient Egyptians had an enormous interest in the circumpolar stars, which they called the "imperishables," and which, according to the Pyramid Texts, the king was to join after death. In 2476 B.C., the brightest of the circumpolar stars, Kochab and Mizar, circled the North Pole, and a line drawn between them would have intersected due north. To find true north, an Egyptian surveyor would simply have had to hold up a plumb line at the right time of night, when the stars lay one above the other, and waited for them to line up exactly. By marking several points on the ground, a line could be drawn to indicate true north. Modern astronomers can track the ancient positions of these stars, which changed according to the wobble of the earth's axis; the rest of the Old Kingdom pyramids deviate to different degrees from true north, corresponding to the gradual drift in alignment of these two stars. It will be interesting, when we finish clearing the base of the third pyramid at Giza, to test Spence's theory there.

Yet another possible technique of finding north involves using the sun rather than stars. A long pole is set into the ground and made perfectly vertical through the use of a plumb line. The shadow cast by this pole about three hours before noon is marked, and a circle is drawn using the length of this shadow as the radius and the pole as the center. At about three hours after noon, the shadow cast by the sun will once again be the right length to intersect this circle. By bisecting the angle created by the intersection of the two shadow lines, it is possible to find true north. However, this method is less accurate than the stellar method and would not account for the variations in accuracy observed over the course of the Old Kingdom.

A foundation ceremony, known as the "stretching of the cord" (perhaps referring to the method of orienting the pyramid), would have been held to celebrate the laying out of the pyramid to the cardinal points. This festival would have involved the entire country and included music, dancing, and enormous quantities of food. The king was mythically assisted in this ceremony by a goddess of writing and measurement named Seshat, one of whose titles, seen in the Pyramid Texts, was "mistress of building." Another important ceremony was the sacrifice of an animal. It was butchered, then pieces were placed on the four corners of the foundation and covered with clean sand, along with other items such as offering vessels, small tablets recording the name of the owner of the pyramid, and models of the tools used in its construction. Such foundation deposits have not been found at Giza, but we have other examples from the Old Kingdom, and it is likely that these rites date back to very early times.

Through several papyri that have survived the ravages of time, we know the Egyptians had a very effective working knowledge of mathematics. They were not able, as far as we know, to formulate complex theorems, but they were able to use arithmetic and geometry to make extremely accurate measurements. They understood the concept of the number one, and could calculate the area of a triangle, square, or circle. Thus it was possible for them, using basic mathematical and simple engineering principles, to plan the Great Pyramid to an extraordinary degree of accuracy.

Once an exact north–south axis had been mapped, the base of the pyramid could be laid out. Evidence found around the Great Pyramid itself, and around the southernmost small queen's pyramid, provides a relatively clear idea of the engineering techniques used. First, a north–south reference line was extended along one side of the pyramid (probably the west). From one corner, a square with angles of precisely 90 degrees was laid out. There are several ways in which the surveyors could have determined these right angles accurately: by using a set square, examples of which are known from later periods of Egyptian history; by using a Pythagorean triangle; or by using intersecting arcs. The remains of postholes along the east and north sides of the Great Pyramid suggest that a reference line was strung outside the base area itself, so that accurate measurements could be maintained along the length of each side. The architects were extremely careful, perhaps due to lessons learned at Dahshur, and the four sides are equal to within twenty centimeters.

When Khufu's architects arrived at Giza, the area of the plateau where his pyramid was to be built sloped significantly. The base of the pyramid was to be 230 meters (755 feet) square—about thirteen acres, vaster than any pyramid built either before or after. A slope of 51 degrees and 52 minutes was planned, which would bring the finished pyramid to an astonishing height of over 147 meters (482 feet), approximately the height of a thirty-story building. In order to create a level surface on which to set this monumental structure, large amounts of bedrock—between seven and ten meters' (thirty-three feet) worth—were quarried away around a core that was left standing in the center. The tools and methods used by the ancient quarrymen to carve out this rock were simple but effective: holes were cut into the rock with copper chisels. Using hammers of stone, wooden stakes were inserted into these holes and then soaked with water. The expansion of the wood split the rock along natural fault lines, so that it could be extracted more easily from its bed.

Around the base of the low core of bedrock, a platform, made primarily of fine white limestone imported from the quarries at Tura (across the river and to the south), was built. This platform was carefully leveled to provide an accurate foundation for the pyramid. It was once believed that the leveling technique used channels of water, whereby an absolutely level horizontal line could be formed by marking the upper limit of the water within the channel. However, it would have been very difficult to transport the amount of water needed and to keep it from evaporating before it could be measured. It is more likely that a simple square level was used. This is an A-shaped instrument, with legs of equal length and a crossbar with its exact center marked. A plumb bob is hung from the point at which the legs join. When the plumb line crosses the center mark on the crossbar, then the surface on which the square is set is level. In fact, the southeast corner of the Great Pyramid is about two centimeters (0.79 inches) higher than the northwest corner, which would be hard to explain if the water method had been used, but is well within the margin of error if a wooden square level was used.

Once the platform and the outcropping had been carefully prepared, and the foundation ceremony performed, work on the pyramid could begin in earnest. A quarry was identified about two hundred meters (656 feet) south of the pyramid. A ramp was built stretching from this quarry to the southwest corner of the pyramid base; in the 1990s, during clearance work around the modern road that encircles the Great Pyramid, we found two sections of this ramp and were able to reconstruct its original course. It was built of mud brick, mud, and stone rubble, and was about three meters (about ten feet) wide. From the end of this straight ramp, which would have risen slightly as it ran to the pyramid, a spiral ramp would have wound its way around the four faces of the pyramid, rising as the pyramid itself rose. A new theory, proposed by French architect Jean-Pierre Houdin, suggests that this spiral ramp actually lay just *inside* the outer face of the pyramid.

Back at the quarry, wide channels were excavated through the bedrock, and narrower channels were carved into the stone left behind in order to subdivide it into the blocks to be used in the pyramid core. Once a block had been separated from the mother stone, the workmen used long wooden levers to pry it from its bed, after which it was placed on a wooden sledge and dragged up the construction ramp to the pyramid site. Modern experiments have determined that ten to twelve men can drag a two-ton block up an incline, using ropes for purchase and water as a lubricant.

It seems as if the pyramid was built one layer at a time, rising slowly to the sky. As best as can be reconstructed, the core blocks were put in place and gaps filled with packing material (such as smaller stones), and then the casing stones were put into place. The casing was of a finer, whiter limestone that was brought to Giza from Tura. Bosses were left on the exterior faces of these blocks in order to render them easier to handle. It seems as though only the bottom and one side of the casing blocks were prepared before they were put into place; the second side and top were finished off in situ. A line was engraved into the top of the casing block to mark the point at which the exterior sloping face would begin; this would serve as a reference later, when this face was smoothed to create a flat, gleaming coating of white. As the pyramid rose, the builders used simple diagonals to make sure that the structure stayed square and properly oriented.

As the pyramid began to rise, a sloping passageway was carved into the bedrock below the pyramid, heading from north to south along a line 23 meters (76 feet) east of the north–south axis. The entrance to this passageway begins above ground level in the north face of the pyramid and slopes down for most of its length, until it levels off and then leads to a roughly cut rectangular chamber. This was originally planned as the chamber in which the king would be buried. The pyramid above, in the shape of the sacred benben, would have served to guide the transfigured spirit of the king to the sky. However, this chamber was never completed, and its walls are still rough and unfinished. A passage leads south from the south wall; this was also left incomplete and leads nowhere. It may originally have been meant as the beginning of a corridor to a second chamber that was never built.

While the underground passages and chambers were being carved and the lowest courses of the pyramid were being laid, the other elements of the complex would also have been begun. Around the pyramid, a wall about three meters (about ten feet) high of stone rubble was planned; some scholars believe that a small open shrine was built against the center of the eastern face within this wall. The upper, or mortuary, temple was to lie to the east of the pyramid, outside the inner enclosure wall. This was to be a small chapel, with a foundation of basalt and walls of fine limestone. Two pits, in the shape of large boats, were planned, one to the north and the other to the south of the mortuary temple. Against the eastern face of the mortuary temple, a causeway was begun that would run all the way to the edge of the floodplain, where a valley temple would mark the entrance to the complex. North of the causeway, near its upper end, a third boat pit dedicated to Hathor would be cut.

One of the first priorities for the builders was to complete the harbor that lay at the foot of the valley temple, connected to the main canal of Menes by a series of smaller channels. Through these waterways supplies, equipment, material (such as the fine limestone from Tura), and personnel would be delivered to the pyramid complex. The palace and administrative city lay nearby.

Back on the high plateau, Khufu planned three subsidiary pyramids for his queens. Tradition would have dictated placing these to the south of the main pyramid, but the construction ramp from the quarry was in the way, so they were laid out to the east instead. Each of these small pyramids was to have its own chapel and miniature boat pit. A small cult pyramid, under which would lie a miniature version of the burial chambers of Khufu, was to rise to the east of the main pyramid, north of the causeway.

South of the last small pyramid, Khufu's architects planned an area of workshops. It is here that the statues and reliefs needed for the temples would have been carved and polished, where the ritual tools used in important ceremonies would have been made. In another area, the place where the king's body was to be mummified was prepared. Much farther to the south, at the point where a great wadi cut through the Mokattam formation and marked the southern limit of the plateau, a monumental wall, known today as the Wall of the Crow, was built to mark the edge of the sacred space. Beyond this wall lay houses, bakeries, and workshops to shelter, feed, and equip the people responsible for the actual work of building the Great Pyramid. I believe that there were actually two distinct villages here: one of simple huts for the workmen who came from all over the country to labor in the service of their king and a second settlement of more elaborate houses for the artisans and supervisors in the permanent employ of the royal house. To the west of the workmen's community, on the slopes and at the foot of the plateau that lies south of the Wall of the Crow, a necropolis was founded, where the artisans, minor officials, and workmen responsible for the construction of the pyramid and their families would be buried.

An enormous number of architects, engineers, overseers, and workers had to be mobilized from the very beginning of Khufu's reign. In addition to the limestone quarry opened on the Giza plateau itself, expeditions had to be sent to various far-flung quarries to secure the different types of stone needed for the pyramid complex. Fine white limestone, as we have seen, came from Tura. The principal use of this stone was for the outer casing of the pyramid, to transform it from a series of rough steps into a smooth surface of gleaming white. Limestone from Tura also served as the surface on which the reliefs that were to decorate the temples and causeway were carved, and it was also used for statues. Stonemasons' marks from the 4th Dynasty have been found in this quarry; a huge tunnel reaching in some cases to a height of ten meters (thirty-three feet) and plunging to a depth of up to fifty meters (164 feet) attests to the huge amounts of stone taken from this site.

Hard greenish-gray basalt for the pavement of the temples came from the Faiyum and Bahariya oases; Egyptian alabaster came from the Middle Egyptian site of Hatnub. Diorite was brought from the western deserts of Nubia, northwest of Toshka, a distance of about 750 miles from Giza. Cedarwood, used for funerary boats, furniture, and other objects, came from the mountains of Lebanon through the coastal port of Byblos. The beautiful pink granite that Khufu chose for the lining of his burial chamber and for his sarcophagus was quarried at Aswan, at the southern border of Egypt. Copper and turquoise were mined in the Sinai, and gold was found in the southern deserts.

All this quarrying required a great deal of manpower and organization. The tools used were simple: stone pounders and hammers, copper picks and chisels, wooden levers; thus simply extracting the stone required many man-hours. One ancient scene from a site near the royal quarry of Tura gives us a good picture of how the actual transport was carried out: it shows a huge block of limestone on a wooden sledge being drawn by three pairs of oxen. The roadway from the quarry to the Nile, where the blocks were loaded onto a ship, was prepared with mud and water. The raw materials had then to be transported to Giza, where

they were brought into the harbor and delivered to the foot of the pyramid complex. Soldiers were needed to guard the sites, especially those
that lay outside the traditional borders of Egypt. Scenes in the Sinai
mines from Khufu's reign depict the king, as his father had done before
him, using his royal mace to smite the Bedouin who attacked his expedition. We also have a scene from a pyramid causeway of the following
dynasty (c. 2506 B.C.), found recently during Supreme Council of Antiquities (SCA) work at the site of Abusir, south of Giza, which depicts
a group of emaciated Bedouin being brought to court to be judged before the royal council; it has been proposed that this group of wretchedly
miserable men had attacked the royal quarrying expedition.

Thus from the beginning of his reign, Khufu mobilized a huge
workforce to build his pyramid complex. He must have been very fortunate in that many of his artisans, overseers, and workmen would have
already gained a great deal of experience working on the pyramids of his
father, Sneferu, and thus would have made the move to Giza easily and
applied their hard-earned expertise to the new project. Our current excavations to the south of the Wall of the Crow, where the men and
women responsible for the Great Pyramid would have lived, worked, and
been buried, are shedding new light on Khufu's enormous achievement.
We are learning a great deal about the common folk, the people who
made up the lower levels of the pyramid that was Egyptian society. We
will learn more about these men and women in Part Four, when we
meet the pyramid builders.

Chapter Seven

Revolution in Year Five

Work on the new pyramid and its complex was progressing rapidly, and things were

going well. Hemiunu brought his reports to the king each day, recounting the work

done, the payments made, and reviewing their progress. But as the fifth anniversary

of the royal coronation approached, the vizier could sense that something was

troubling his king. One day, Khufu called Hemiunu to his chambers. Seated in a

simple chair of precious wood inlaid with his names and titles, his head covered by

the nemes head scarf, the ruler of Egypt greeted his vizier, who prostrated himself

on the floor, then stood at attention. "I have been thinking," the king told him. "I

have been studying the ancient texts, and I believe we have wandered from the path

of ma'at, *and neglected the true will of the gods."*

We do not know exactly why, but in the fifth year of his reign, Khufu had the layout of his complex modified. The subterranean burial chamber was abandoned, its rock fill only partly removed, and a new passage, ascending through the body of the pyramid, was begun. This was to lead to a room high within the pyramid, now known by the misnomer of

Queen's Chamber. Planned either at the same time or as another modification of the interior plan, the ascending passage was extended into a marvel of engineering, the corbeled grandeur of the Grand Gallery, leading to a third chamber, the King's Chamber, in which the granite sarcophagus of the king was placed. The upper temple was enlarged, and the positions of the northernmost small pyramid and the cult pyramid modified accordingly; the cuttings which had been begun for these monuments were left unfinished in the bedrock. The upper entrance to the causeway also had to be moved; and in order to link it with the valley temple, its course had to be modified partway along its route.

These changes were most probably connected with modifications in the royal cult and dogma, a continuation of Sneferu's hypothetical struggle with the priesthood of Re at Heliopolis. Perhaps the priests were putting pressure on the king to grant various requests, and trying to get him to follow the program they had designed for him. Or perhaps Khufu wanted to make certain that the country's wealth was concentrated at Giza, not at Heliopolis. In any case, it is possible that, in the fifth year of his reign, Khufu identified himself as the sun god.

One piece of evidence we have for this change is the name that Khufu chose for his pyramid complex: Akhet Khufu, the horizon of Khufu. Thus he identified himself directly with the sun god—by moving his burial chamber to a position high within the core of his pyramid, he would rise and set within the sacred symbol of the benben, just as Re would rise and set within the larger cosmos. Before the reign of his father, Sneferu, Egyptian kings had been buried beneath the earth. At Dahshur, and here again at Giza, the king became Re, rising above the horizon.

Much of the information we have on Khufu's cult must be extrapolated from what we know about the function of his pyramid complex, which is itself difficult to reconstruct. The decoration of the temples and causeways, which would tell us a great deal, was torn from the walls and shattered into pieces several centuries after Khufu's death. Thus we must attempt to understand the fragments that remain by looking at the architecture and comparable decoration found in situ in other Old Kingdom pyramid complexes, and by using written sources such as the Pyramid Texts, found inscribed in the interior chambers of later pyramids.

What remains to us from the decoration of Khufu's complex has been recovered primarily from scattered fragments found around the upper temple, causeway, and queens' pyramids, and from the interior fill of the 12th Dynasty pyramid of Amenemhet I (c. 1991–1962 B.C.) at Lisht. Scholars have struggled for many years to figure out where these reliefs might have originally been located within Khufu's pyramid complex.

The complex was meant to be entered from the east, through the lower, or valley, temple that lay in the floodplain at the foot of the plateau. From 1988 to 1994, while soundings were being taken and trenches were being dug to lay new sewer pipes under the suburb of Nazlet el-Samman as part of the Sphinx Conservation Project, the remains of this temple were discovered on the site of a large private villa near the Mansouria canal. Unfortunately, we were already having difficulties with the residents of this area, so we did not request that this villa be moved. We were able to trace the north-south length of the basalt pavement that had once served as the floor of the temple, but we were not able to excavate its entire width because it ran underneath the villa. In any event, knowing its location is vital to understanding the archaeology of the complex, and we now know that it was paved with basalt, which is basically black but gives off a greenish reflection and symbolizes fertility.

A number of the fragments recovered from Lisht may have belonged to this temple, including depictions of personified estates, both male and female, bringing offerings. Similar processions were found in Sneferu's lower temple; and this was the entrance to the complex, where the actual offerings from Khufu's estates would have been delivered. Another fragment includes Khufu's titulary, with the wing of a hawk hovering above. Beside Khufu's cartouche is the head of a foreigner, and it has been suggested that a statue of the king stood below this relief.

Another scene shows Khufu with foreigners. This is the first scene of its type known from a pyramid complex. When such scenes are found in complexes of the 5th and 6th Dynasties, they are in the lower temple or causeway, and would probably have served to help mark the limits of the sacred space—foreigners are considered embodiments of chaos, which must be kept at bay, at the fringes of the Egyptian world, and thus, symbolically, at the edges of the sacred space. The complex was, at one level, a model of the Egyptian cosmos; and by showing the king triumphant over his enemies, the proper order of the universe was magically maintained.

Another fragment that most likely belonged to the lower temple depicts ships under sail, and yet another bears a hieroglyphic inscription and part of a boat made from papyrus reeds. This would probably have been used by the king on sporting expeditions into the marshes; scenes depicting these activities also have a level of meaning associating the king with Horus maintaining order over the forces of chaos, represented by the wildlife of the marshes, which constantly threatened the Egyptian world. From Lisht we have another scene that may come from the lower temple; this one shows members of the royal suite and an attendant with a sunshade.

Overall, the primary function of the lower temple seems to have been to receive offerings from the royal estates and to represent the place in which the king was worshipped as Horus, responsible for maintaining the proper order of the Egyptian cosmos.

Khufu's causeway led up toward the plateau from a doorway in the southern wall of the valley temple. It ran southwest for about a third of its length, and then bent to run more directly east until it reached the upper temple. Enough of this causeway remained in the fifth century B.C. for Herodotus to be able to describe it as a huge roofed structure decorated with birds and stars.

Many fragments from Giza and Lisht are likely to belong to this causeway. A fragment bearing the king's titles and a representation of Libyan captives, illustrating the king's power over foreigners, may come from the lower end. A procession of oxen bearing foreign offerings or captives could have been in the central section of the causeway (the forces of chaos have now been defeated and tamed and thus can be brought symbolically into the sacred space). Depictions of royal estates, also seen in the lower temple, may have been repeated in the causeway. Another fragment, perhaps from the upper end of the causeway, shows the stern of a boat being paddled.

Much of the decoration of the causeway repeats the decoration of the lower temple. Like the lower temple, the causeway served as both entrance and protection for the inner complex. In passing through the causeway, one would make the transition from the outer world—the fringes of the cosmos, where order had to be maintained constantly over the forces of chaos—into the inner world, the protected sacred space.

The basalt pavement of the upper temple still lies at the eastern foot of the pyramid, and its basic plan can be traced in the foundations that remain. The sanctuary was oblong; the ceremonies carried out here would probably have been offering rituals for the cult of the deceased king as the sun god, Re. In the surrounding magazines would have been the items needed for these rituals, such as the tools for the Opening of the Mouth, as well as furniture and funerary equipment. The temple also had an open court. According to one reconstruction of the badly destroyed sanctuary, Khufu's upper temple was the first to contain five niches, perhaps four niches to house statues representing the king as Re and the fifth niche for a cult statue of Hathor. There were several royal statue fragments found in various locations around the complex as a whole that may have come from this temple.

The use of basalt here, as in the lower temple, carries connotations of fertility. White and yellow alabaster (really a form of translucent limestone known more accurately as travertine or calcite) were also used.

The name of the area where this material was quarried, Hatnub, means "house of gold," and emphasizes the king's relationship with the sun god Re, whose identifying material was this precious metal.

It is likely that only the court and portico of the upper temple were decorated with scenes. Many of the fragments recovered from both Giza and Lisht bear representations of the various ceremonies associated with the Sed festival, and these seem to have been the primary types of scenes used to decorate this temple. Dominating many of these scenes is the king himself. In some, he is seen in a short kilt, performing some of the Sed festival ceremonies. One scene depicts the god Wepwawet, an important mortuary god, in human form with the head of a canine. This particular scene has no parallel in other pyramid temples.

Another scene, probably from the wall of the court, represents a goddess, labeled "Meret of the Upper Egyptian lands," who receives the king when he approaches the temple to perform the ceremonies at the Sed festival. As a goddess of music, Meret is linked with Hathor, who is also associated with music. Also depicted in this scene are several priests; and an adjoining block shows six members of the king's entourage, three of whom are "controllers of the palace," the other three of whom bear other courtly and priestly titles. Another fragmentary scene, found built into a staircase in Islamic Cairo, depicts a white hippopotamus. A similar scene occurs in the hall of Pepi II's mortuary temple (built c. 2300–2206 B.C.), and thus the Cairo scene may have been in a similar location in Khufu's temple.

Based on scenes found in other pyramid temples, the portico may also have contained scenes showing the king making offerings to various gods. However, the fact is that no fragments of such scenes have been found. This may be due to accidents of preservation, but may also be a result of Khufu's cult, in which Khufu himself was a god and the equal of the other gods.

Unique to Khufu's complex is the arrangement of his boat pits. There are five of these: one alongside the causeway, two flanking the

mortuary temple, and two to the south of the pyramid. The two southern boat pits are separated by a wall of bedrock that lies on the north-
south axis of the Great Pyramid, and they differ from the others in that
they are rectangular rather than boat shaped.

The southern boat pits were discovered in 1954 by Egyptian archaeologist Kamal el-Mallakh. The eastern pit was covered by forty-one slabs
of limestone weighing about fifteen tons each, nine of which bore
quarry marks. Among these were eighteen cartouches of Khufu's son
and successor Djedefre, showing that he had taken responsibility for his
father's funeral. When he opened the pit, el-Mallakh found the dismantled pieces of a full-size wooden boat made of cedar and acacia. Resting
on top of the wooden planks of the boat were a layer of mats and ropes,
an instrument made of flint, and some small pieces of white plaster. In
addition to the pieces of the boat itself, many of which were tied together with ropes, there were a number of other items: twelve oars, ten
for rowing and two for steering, each of which was made of a single
piece of wood; fifty-eight poles; three cylindrical columns; and five
doors. In total, the pit contained 651 artifacts.

It took expert conservator Hag Ahmed Youssef many years to preserve and reconstruct the ancient boat, which is now housed inside a
rather hideous museum over its original pit. The reconstructed boat is
about forty-three meters (141 feet) long and six meters (twenty feet)
wide. The prow is a tall pole topped with a round wooden disk. Amid-
ships is a roofed cabin that was designed for the magical and eternal use
of the king. The function of this boat is still hotly debated: el-Mallakh
believed it was a solar boat, designed for the use of Khufu as Re in the
afterlife. Other scholars believe it was one of the boats used for his funeral, and was buried after this ceremony had been completed. One
thing that might help decide between at least these two possibilities is to
determine whether or not this boat had ever traveled on the river. The
preponderance of the data, including evidence that it was built near
where it was buried and the fact that it was never painted or decorated,

suggests that it was buried without being used and had a symbolic rather than a practical function. However, there is no scholarly agreement on this point.

The western of the two southern boat pits is still covered by twenty limestone slabs, but a camera inserted into the pit by the National Geographic Society in 1988 found that it contains yet another dismantled wooden boat. The Japanese have done some conservation work on this pit and have covered it with a shelter; this second boat will be excavated and reconstructed as soon as we have sufficient funds to do so properly and safely.

There are many different theories about the functions of Khufu's five boat pits. Similar pits and large model boats have been found associated with a number of royal and high elite complexes from the 1st through the 5th Dynasties. Recently, David O'Connor, an American Egyptologist who has dedicated much of his life to excavations at Abydos, uncovered fourteen wooden boats encased with mud plaster and equipped with stone anchors, moored near the valley enclosure of the last king of the 2nd Dynasty, Khasekhemwy. The exact functions of boats and boat pits found in mortuary contexts are still being debated, but they seem certainly to have had purposes both practical (boats were the primary means of transportation in ancient Egypt) and symbolic (gods were also thought to travel in boats).

For Khufu's complex, I believe that the pits next to the mortuary temple were for the king as Horus to control the Two Lands: the northern boat would be for Lower Egypt, and the southern boat for Upper Egypt. The boats south of the pyramid were for the king as Re: one represented the day barque, in which the king as sun god traveled from east to west across the sky, and the other was the night barque, in which the god traveled from west to east through the netherworld in order to be reborn each morning. The fifth boat, along the causeway, might have been for the queen as Hathor or might once have held the boat used to bring Khufu's body to its final resting place.

When the layout of the mortuary temple was changed, the location of the northernmost queen's pyramid had to be moved several meters to the west. By choosing to bury his most important queens in pyramids, Khufu was including them in his cult. As we have seen, each major queen was associated with the goddess Hathor; in the Old Kingdom, she was also known as the lady of the sycomore, a tree that grew in the Memphite region. There are many women buried at Giza who bear the title "priestess of Hathor"; it is these women who would have maintained the cults of the royal queens, worshipping them and presenting them with the offerings and rituals they needed to function eternally in the cosmos. Two of the three queens' pyramids have small boat pits carved into the bedrock along their southern faces; these boat pits would have served as magical transportation for each queen as Hathor as she followed the king as Horus or Re in his efforts to maintain the proper order of the Egyptian world.

The next-to-last major element of the pyramid complex proper was the cult pyramid. Since one had never been found, it was assumed for a long time that Khufu had no cult pyramid, and the question of why this important element had not been included in his complex remained a major problem for scholars. The unfinished cuttings north of the causeway were thought perhaps to be associated with such a pyramid, but the superstructure had never been built. And then, in 1991—while I was recovering in the hospital from a heart attack—my team at Giza, which was working to clear the area east of the Great Pyramid as part of our site management plan, came across its remains. Only the substructure and scattered blocks from the superstructure remained, but we found enough to reconstruct it as a pyramid with a base of 10.7 square meters (115 square feet). One day, as I was supervising the excavations, I put my hand on a limestone block and realized that it was the capstone of the small pyramid!

The interior of the pyramid is very simple: a sloping passage entered from the center of the north face leads to a rectangular chamber, oriented east-west. This chamber was empty but for several miscellaneous stones. This structure appears to have been built hurriedly, perhaps even after the death of the king.

The culmination of Khufu's complex is the Great Pyramid itself, one of the most astonishing monuments ever built. Theories, many of them completely ridiculous and unfounded, about its function and its builders abound; it has fascinated mankind for centuries, and interest in it does not seem to be abating. The pyramid still holds some mysteries, but we do know a great deal and are learning more all the time. Khufu's pyramid was not built by men from Atlantis or aliens from outer space. The archaeological evidence demonstrates beyond any sort of reasonable doubt that it was built by the ancient Egyptians in about c. 2506 B.C., give or take a century or so. It was designed to serve as the tomb of the Egyptian king, and, perhaps even more important, to act as the focus of his cult.

As discussed previously, one of the most unusual features of this pyramid is that there is a system of chambers and passages within the core of the pyramid itself, rather than below the superstructure, as is more usual. This is the case for only one other king, Khufu's father, Sneferu, and is most likely connected with the cults of these two rulers as the sun god Re. The original burial chamber lay underneath the pyramid, and it was only with the changes of plan in the fifth year of Khufu's reign that chambers were moved to within the pyramid itself. The official in charge of the pyramid—perhaps Hemiunu or perhaps one of the other great men buried at Giza or Meidum—was a brilliant architect and engineer, as evidenced by the extraordinary degree of accuracy in the alignment, layout, and construction of this pyramid. Building within the superstructure itself was a remarkable feat of engineering, requiring careful planning and flawless execution. For example, above the King's Chamber, the highest room within the pyramid, the architects left five relieving chambers, designed to take some of the weight of the pyramid above off the empty space below. By the next reign, perhaps for both religious and technical reasons, the burial chambers were back underneath the superstructure, where they stayed for the remainder of the history of pyramid building.

Some earlier pyramids had contained decoration, but Sneferu had left the interior chambers of his pyramid uninscribed. Khufu followed his example and chose to line both upper chambers of his pyramid with polished, undecorated granite. Khufu's plain granite sarcophagus was set into the floor of the King's Chamber, and it is generally assumed that the king was buried here.

There are a number of other anomalies associated with Khufu's pyramid. It is the only pyramid to contain "air shafts," mysterious tunnels, each about twenty centimeters square (three square inches), that lead outward from the north and south walls of the two upper chambers of his pyramid. The two shafts in the uppermost chamber reach the outside, but those in the lower chamber do not. The two shafts in the Queen's Chamber had been discovered in the nineteenth century, but the technology of the time did not allow much investigation. The man who first explored them (an Englishman named Waynman Dixon) did find a small bronze hook (similar in shape to instruments used for the Opening of the Mouth ceremony), a granite ball, and a piece of resinous wood inside. In 1993, as part of my site management plan, I asked the German Institute to help us clean the air shafts in the King's Chamber so that we could install a ventilation system to help keep down the humidity inside the pyramid. Robotics expert Rudolph Gantenbrink designed a series of robots, named Wepwawet after an ancient god of the dead, small enough to fit inside the shafts. After the shafts in the upper chamber were finished and the system installed, we sent the robot into the northern shaft of the Queen's Chamber. To our surprise, the shaft turned sharply to the west after about eight meters (twenty-seven feet), and the robot could go no further. In the southern shaft, Wepwawet was able to proceed for sixty-three meters (208 feet), until it was stopped by a mysterious limestone slab with two copper handles that blocked the passage.

In September of 2002, the SCA was finally prepared—with the help of the National Geographic Society and a new robot, named the Pyramid Rover—to look beyond the peculiar limestone slab. The great moment was broadcast live to an international audience. We drilled a small hole through the door so that we could send a camera behind it: twenty-one centimeters (eight inches) from the first door is a second, which looked as if it was screening or covering something. We later sent the Pyramid Rover into the northern shaft, where it was able to negotiate the turn and discover a second limestone slab with copper handles, sixty-three meters (208 feet) into the shaft, the same distance as in the southern shaft. I expect that we will find a wall behind this slab, just as we found in the southern shaft. We will be sending a new robot into the southern shaft, to see what lies beyond the second door.

One of the two air shafts in the King's Chamber is located on the central axis of the southern face of the pyramid and is at right angles to the east-west axis of the two boats. It may be that the soul of the king was thought to be able to magically travel through this air shaft in order to board his boat. The shaft also points toward Orion, identified by the Egyptians with the god Osiris. The northern shaft is directed toward the circumpolar stars and most likely represents a magical path on which the soul of the king would have traveled to join these stars, his fellow gods. Interpretation of the shafts in the Queen's Chamber must wait until we have explored them further and coaxed them into giving up their mysteries.

The theory of Khufu as Re in his lifetime must remain, for the time being, unproven, but several other pieces of evidence point clearly to the conclusion that Khufu carried out some sort of religious revolution. As mentioned above, the fragmentary wall reliefs from Khufu's complex do not include images that show the king giving offerings to the gods. This may be due to accidents of preservation, but it is also possible that, as Khufu was now himself a god, it was no longer appropriate for him to be shown making offerings to other gods. Khufu's son and successor,

Djedefre, was the first Egyptian king to bear the epithet "son of Re." Djedefre's successor, Khafre, another son of Khufu, claimed this epithet also, and it became a standard part of the titulary of the Egyptian king. I believe the Great Sphinx itself represents Khafre worshipping his father Khufu as the sun god. Thus Khufu's new cult may have been the first religious revolution in ancient Egypt; perhaps he even dismissed the priests of Heliopolis and organized his own cult at Giza.

After the fall of the Old Kingdom in about 2165 B.C., Khufu's temples were destroyed, the reliefs ripped from the walls and shattered. Khafre's many statues were also smashed. The type of destruction reflected in the archaeological record suggests more than simple theft. It is possible that the religious changes instituted by Khufu and followed by his sons led eventually to a backlash and a resurgence of the power of the priesthood of Re.

There is a remarkable lack of statuary from Khufu's reign. Although several unidentifiable fragments were found at Giza, there is only one certain image of the king himself, a small statuette of ivory found at Abydos in a temple to the mortuary god Khenty-imentiu. However, the area in which it was found dates to later than the 4th Dynasty: I believe that the statuette itself was carved in the 26th Dynasty, when a cult to Khufu flourished. Only a few full-figure private statues, of the types common both before and after Khufu's time, can be dated to his reign. The exceptions, such as a seated statue of his vizier Hemiunu, belong to very high officials. Another of Khufu's viziers, Ankhhaf, was permitted only a bust. The principal type of sculpture in the round that has been preserved from this period is the reserve head; a majority of these (about thirty-seven are known), in fact, may date to Khufu's reign. These represent only the head and neck of the tomb owner, and no one is certain of their function (see p. 100). In any case, they are another indication of changes during the reign of Khufu, perhaps to accommodate his new cult.

Chapter Eight

Ruthless Monarch or Great Scientist?

King Khufu sat in his audience chamber, contemplating eternity. His pyramid continued to rise swiftly, gangs of well-fed, healthy men toiling to haul the huge stones up the ramps that corkscrewed around its still-hidden face. The royal sculptors were busy carving the acres of reliefs that would adorn his temples. But still, he was not satisfied. Had he understood the will of the gods correctly? Was the all-important arrangement of the chambers within his pyramid tomb correct? There was a manuscript in the library at On that he wanted to see for himself. He would no longer trust his fate to those foolish priests. No one could understand the words of the ancients better than he, and it was time to take matters completely into his own hands.

*I*t is hard, even at a distance of a generation or two, to reconstruct the personalities and characters of important historical figures. History, as they say, is written by the victors; without unbiased contemporary sources, which are almost impossible to find, a ruthless dictator with a great propaganda machine can be remembered by posterity as a benevolent monarch, or a brilliant and just ruler can be portrayed as an evil monster. We have no contemporary accounts from the reign of Khufu. By the time of Herodotus, almost two thousand years after Khufu's death, he had acquired a reputation as a tyrant:

> [Khufu] brought the country into all sorts of misery. He closed all the temples, then, not content with excluding his subjects from the practice of their religion, compelled them without exception to labour as slaves for his own advantage. (Herodotus, *The Histories*, Book II [trans. by Aubrey de Selincourt])

Herodotus also reports that the central of the queens' pyramids was built by Khufu's daughter, who, when the king ran short of money, was sent to work as a prostitute to refill his treasury. In addition to the fee she charged on her father's behalf, she asked each of her customers to give her a block of stone, with which she built her own small pyramid! According to the reports given to Herodotus, which he recounted faithfully, the Egyptians of the 5th century A.D., or at least the ancient tour guides who haunted the pyramids, did not remember the builder of the Great Pyramid kindly.

An Egyptian priest named Manetho, who compiled a history of the past kings of Egypt in the second century B.C. with access to many more-reliable sources than Herodotus might have had, gives no opinions about Khufu's personality but reports that this king wrote an important book, which was highly regarded throughout Egyptian history.

Closest in time to Khufu's own day is the Westcar Papyrus, to which we have already been introduced. This series of stories, written down in about the 12th Dynasty, depicts a king in search of knowledge, fascinated by the arcane. The entire story, at least what remains to us, is set in Khufu's court: the king's sons take turns telling their father stories about extraordinary events that have taken place in the time of his ancestors. After the tale of Sneferu and the rowing girls recounted by his son

Baufre, Prince Dedefhor stands up to speak. After noting that all the tales told so far have been about people no longer among the living, and whose truth cannot be guaranteed, he announces that Khufu has, as one of his own subjects, a magician named Djedi living in Djed-Sneferu (Meidum). "He is a man of a hundred and ten years who eats five hundred loaves of bread, half an ox for meat, and drinks one hundred jugs of beer to this very day. He can join a severed head. He can make a lion walk behind him, its leash on the ground. And he knows the number of the secret chambers of the sanctuary of Thoth."*

According to the story, Khufu was most intrigued by the mention of the secret chambers of Thoth (god of writing and wisdom), for which he had been searching so that he could replicate them in his own temple. He sends Dedefhor south to fetch Djedi, and we are treated to a rare glimpse of an ancient Egyptian traveling in style: "After the ships had been moored to the shore, he traveled overland seated in a carrying chair of ebony, the poles of which were of *seshnedjem*—wood plated with gold." The prince finds Djedi lying on a mat in the courtyard of his house, getting a massage, and invites him to Giza. Djedi, clearly expecting a long stay at the capital, asks that his children and his books be brought along, and the entire entourage proceeds to the royal barges and thence to Khufu's palace.

The king and the magician meet, and Khufu asks immediately whether or not it is true that Djedi can join a severed head. Djedi replies that he can, and Khufu asks that a prisoner be brought and executed so that the old man can perform his magic. Djedi objects, exclaiming, "But not to a human being, O king, my lord! Surely it is not permitted to do such a thing to the noble cattle!" They settle on a goose, and after Djedi rejoins its head to its body, he performs the same trick with a bird (probably a crane) and an ox.

*Translation from Miriam Lichtheim, *Ancient Egyptian Literature*.

Then Khufu gets down to serious business: "It was also said that you know the number of the secret chambers of the sanctuary of Thoth." Djedi replies that he does not know the number himself but knows where the information is, namely inside a chest of flint in a building in On (Heliopolis). Khufu orders him to bring it, but Djedi tells him that it is not he who will bring it but the eldest of the three children who are in the womb of a woman named Ruddedet, wife of a high priest of Re, continuing: "He has said concerning them that they will assume this beneficent office [the kingship] in this whole land, and the eldest of them will be high priest in On." Khufu grows sad at this news, and Djedi comforts him, saying: "first your son, then his son, then one of them." Khufu expresses a desire to go to visit the temple of Re when Ruddedet is due to deliver, and Djedi assures him that he will make sure the way is navigable, even though it will be during the summer, and the sand-banks he must traverse will be dry. The king rewards the magician, plac-ing him in the house of Prince Dedefhor and giving him a pension.

The papyrus goes on to relate the birth of the royal children of Ruddedet. This story is particularly fascinating in light of the current theory that Khufu was engaged in a power struggle with the priests of Re. In fact, Khufu's line lasted about another fifty years before the events foretold in hindsight in the Westcar Papyrus came to pass. But the 5th Dynasty, which came to power in about 2513 B.C., had a different rela-tionship to the priests of Heliopolis, and there may be an element of truth in the fantastic tale. The kings of this line built, in addition to their own pyramids, sun temples dedicated to Re, with large, squat obelisks as the foci of the solar cult. Thus the power theoretically wrested by Sne-feru and Khufu from the priesthood of Heliopolis may have been re-gained at this point and a family closely associated with and loyal to them placed on the throne. The tales as a whole have been seen as an attempt to legitimize the 5th Dynasty; however, the papyrus itself, the earliest and only copy we have of what must once have been a popular story, dates from the Hyksos period (around 1600 B.C.), and the ending of the last tale is missing, so the true rationale for these tales escapes us now.

What does this tale tell us about the character of Khufu? Some scholars see the fact that Khufu is willing to have the head of a prisoner cut off just to see if it can be put back on as support for Herodotus's portrayal of him as an evil tyrant. However, this negative view is not really supported by the story itself. In fact, the king does nothing when his courtier scolds him, acceding peacefully to the older man's judgment and accepting his rebuke—certainly not the act of a merciless man! When he hears of the dynasty that will supplant him, he does not rush out and have the woman or her newborn children killed; he bows to fate and rewards the man who has given him the bad news.

It is certainly interesting to speculate about the secret chambers of Thoth—what they might have been and why Khufu was looking for them, or at least was remembered as looking for them. Perhaps a folk memory concerning the unique layout of the interior of his pyramid had survived through the years; certainly this story, combined with Manetho's claim that Khufu had written an important book, presents a portrait of a learned man, interested in the greatness of the past and desirous of conforming to the ideals of *ma'at*.

Chapter Nine

Khufu's Court

Khufu was greatly pleased with his two highest officials, Hemiunu and Ankhhaf,
both of whom he had known all his life and whom he trusted implicitly. He was
worried about his mother, who was getting on in years, but she still maintained an
iron control over the affairs of the harem, not an easy task with his various wives
and sons jockeying for position and power. He was certainly not lacking for
potential heirs! It would be time to name his crown prince soon, and the decision
was difficult. But he comforted himself with the thought that his pyramid was
rising rapidly, reaching to the sky and ensuring his eternal life as a god, regardless
of what happened on the earth after he left it. He had chosen his highest officials
well, and the country was in good hands, her enemies subdued and wealth pouring
into her coffers.

We know from the tomb of a high-ranking government official
named Ranofer, one of whose titles was director of the pyramid city of
Sneferu, that part of the court remained at Djed-Sneferu (Meidum) to

serve the cult of this king. The Abusir Papyri, royal archives from the 5th Dynasty (about 2450 B.C.), also mention Djed-Sneferu, written with the town determinative, thus clearly referring to the town rather than the pyramid. The prince Rahotep and his wife Nofret were buried there, possibly after the accession of Khufu, as were Neferma'at and Atet. Most of the court, however, would have gone with Khufu to Giza, and lived with and worked for the new king there.

Based on the location of Sneferu's pyramid cities, and the well-documented pyramid cities of Menkaure and Queen Khentkawes, the buildings that housed Khufu's administration and sheltered his courtiers should have been located near his valley temple. The great American Egyptologist George Reisner, who spent much of his life excavating at Giza, was the first to suggest that Khufu's pyramid city should be sought under the modern village of Nazlet el-Samman, and indeed, as mentioned previously, glimpses of the larger city associated with his complex were caught in the 1980s and 1990s, while soundings were being taken for the new sewage system. In addition, excavations carried out in 1978 in an area free of modern construction, on a mound east of the plateau and south of Khufu's lower temple, uncovered remains of a Greco-Roman settlement, including many late Roman potsherds. This has been identified with the town of Busiris, known from both Egyptian and classical sources. There is also some evidence for a New Kingdom settlement in the same area: a modern village near Nazlet el-Samman is called el-Harnia, based on the Canaanite name for the Great Sphinx, Haroun. Since people tend to build in the same place, the existence of New Kingdom and Greco-Roman occupations in this area suggests that this is the most likely location for the elite quarters of Khufu's city.

What we know of Khufu's family and administration comes primarily from the tombs of the Giza necropolis; without archives and settlement remains, we must use the words and images of the dead to reconstruct the realities of their lives. There are two major cemeteries here containing tombs belonging to the members of Khufu's family and

Aerial view of the pyramids at Giza, looking from the south. [*Marcello Bertinetti*]

The cemetery of the pyramid builders at Giza, south of the Great Sphinx.
[*Zahi Hawass Library*]

View of the remains of the causeway, mortuary temple, and pyramid of Menkaure.
[*Ronald Dunlap*]

The Great Pyramid of Khufu. [*Marcello Bertinetti*]

Diorite statue of Khafre, his head protected by the Horus falcon, discovered hidden in a pit in his valley temple. [*Kenneth Garrett*]

The Great Sphinx at Giza, an image of Khafre. [*Zahi Hawass Library*]

The royal installation of the pyramid builders at Giza. [*Zahi Hawass Library*]

Aerial view of the pyramid of Menkaure at Giza. [*Marcello Bertinetti*]

The pyramid of Sneferu at Meidum. [*Marcello Bertinetti*]

The pyramid of Sneferu at Meidum,
seen from the fields under cultivation.
[*Giulio Veggi*]

Close-up of Sneferu's cartouche, inscribed on the
belt of a statue from his valley temple at Dahshur.
[*Sandro Vannini*]

Aerial view of the Bent Pyramid of Sneferu at Dahshur. [*Marcello Bertinetti*]

The Bent Pyramid of Sneferu at Dahshur. [*Zahi Hawass Library*]

Statue of Sneferu in the white crown of Upper Egypt, from his valley temple at Dahshur. [*Sandro Vannini*]

Triad of Hathor, Menkaure, and a nome goddess, from Menkaure's valley temple at Giza. [*Sandro Vannini*]

Diorite statue of Khafre, discovered hidden in a pit in his valley temple. [*Sandro Vannini*]

his court. In the cemetery directly east of the Great Pyramid, begun in the fifth year of Khufu's reign, are the tombs of his wives, children, and grandchildren, many of whom were also high officials in his court. In the cemetery west of the Great Pyramid, founded in the twelfth year of his reign, lie other of the great king's officials and priests, including viziers, treasurers, tenant farmers, and those who maintained the royal cult. Both cemeteries were originally laid out in regular rows with streets running between them, as cities of the dead, frozen in stone. These cemeteries continued in use until the end of the Old Kingdom; as time passed, smaller tombs were built around the larger ones, and the original clarity of their plans disappeared beneath the chaos of time, just as must have happened in the cities of the living.

These regularly planned towns of the dead were yet another innovation of Khufu's reign. The beginnings of this practice go back to the 1st Dynasty, when those who served the king in life accompanied him into death. In our current work at Saqqara, clearing and reexcavating some large 1st Dynasty tombs there, we have found two intact subsidiary tombs. In one shaft lay the linen-covered body of a thirty-five-year-old woman whose neck had been broken and who had evidence of blood on her leg; in the other was a wooden chest containing the partially mummified skeleton of a man—our earliest evidence for the practice of mummification. Although the practice of human sacrifice was abandoned in the 2nd Dynasty, family members and retainers continued to be buried in tombs scattered near the burials of their kings throughout the 3rd Dynasty and into the 4th. However, it was Khufu who formalized this arrangement, laying out rows and rows of mastabas for his family and officials. It is a testimony to the power of his personality and cult that so many sought an eternal home in the shadow of his pyramid, his necropolises continuing in use for hundreds of years. His successors, both within the 4th Dynasty and to the end of the Old Kingdom, all have cemeteries associated with their pyramids, but none are as clearly defined or as regularly organized as Khufu's.

The Royal Family

Khufu's immediate family was buried in the Eastern Cemetery, which was laid out on a unified plan. Just east of the Great Pyramid were the pyramids of three queens, which had been planned and begun before the cult change in the fifth year of his reign. As mentioned before, the northernmost pyramid was moved when the funerary temple was expanded. I believe that this pyramid, GI-a, was built for the burial of the queen mother, Hetepheres I.

In 1925, Reis Mahmadien, a photographer working with George Reisner of the Boston Museum of Fine Arts, who was then excavating at Giza, was setting up his tripod to take pictures when he uncovered a limestone slab of the sort that often blocked the entrance to a tomb. Reisner was away at the time, on vacation in the United States, but he returned immediately when he heard the news. Excavations revealed a stairway, twelve steps long, leading to a deep vertical shaft filled to the top with limestone blocks. Near the bottom of the fill, which contained various artifacts and pottery shards, was a sealing (the imprint from a seal) bearing the name of Khufu's mortuary workshop. In the west wall of the shaft was a niche containing the remains of a disturbed offering: three leg bones of a bull wrapped in a reed mat, a horned skull that had been crushed, two wine jars, a limestone boulder, two chips of basalt, and some charcoal.

At the bottom of the shaft was a chamber crammed with extraordinary treasures, now at the Cairo Museum. Many of the items had been made of gilded wood, including a portable pavilion, a bed, two armchairs, and a carrying chair (perhaps just like the one used by Dedefhor in the Westcar Papyrus!). Scattered among these larger items were a curtain box; a leather case for walking sticks; several wooden boxes; some copper tools; and numerous other small objects, including twenty silver bracelets inlaid with turquoise, lapis lazuli, and carnelian, designed to be worn simultaneously on the queen's arms. A square canopic chest with four compartments, holding wrapped packages containing the queen's viscera in a solution of natron and water, was found resting on a small wooden sledge within a sealed recess in the west wall of the burial chamber. Against one wall of the chamber was an alabaster sarcophagus closed with a lid; when this was opened, the casket was found to be empty, and the tomb became one of the great mysteries of Egyptology.

Some of the furniture was inlaid with the names and titles of Sneferu and the name and titles of Hetepheres, who was "mother of the king of Upper and Lower Egypt" and "daughter of the god." Mud sealings from Khufu's workshop were also found in some of the boxes, where they seem to have been thrown after having been wrenched from the objects they had once guarded. The name of Hetepheres and the title "mother of the king" were also inscribed on a vase discovered at Byblos.

How can we explain the mystery of the tomb of Hetepheres (known as Hetepheres I, since several of her royal descendants bore the same name)? Why was there no superstructure above her tomb, why was the burial chamber in such disarray, and most important, why was her body missing?

Here is the scenario that Reisner developed to explain the situation: Hetepheres I died during the early years of Khufu's reign and was buried in style at Dahshur, near her husband. At some point, still during Khufu's reign, robbers broke into her tomb and stole her body. When the king heard that his mother's eternal rest had been disturbed, he had the remains of her burial equipment moved in secret to this hastily dug shaft near his pyramid at Giza. Reisner observed that the side of the empty sarcophagus against the wall of the chamber was damaged, so believed that it must have been broken into elsewhere. In addition, he suggested that the contents of the chamber are reversed in order, as if the first objects taken out of the hypothetical Dahshur tomb were the first placed into the Giza tomb. Forgotten items were thrown down into the body of the shaft at the last minute. Since an offering was made at this new tomb, Khufu must not have known that the body of the queen was missing. Basalt fragments were found inside the offering niche, leading Reisner to conclude that all this took place while the pavement of the upper temple was being laid.

Mark Lehner disagrees with Reisner, noting that robbers would have smashed the sarcophagus lid and taken all the portable objects (the beautiful silver bracelets, for example); he also objects to the idea that such a deep shaft could have been dug in secret, and finds it extremely unlikely that Khufu would have agreed to let his mother be reburied with broken pottery and violated equipment. Pointing out that the style of the Hetepheres shaft dates it to the 3rd Dynasty, so it must have been dug at the latest early in Khufu's reign, he suggests instead that Hetepheres was originally buried in this shaft, dug as part of the original layout of GI-a. A superstructure was started but had to be abandoned when the layout of the upper temple was changed, since it was now in the way. When the three small pyramids were built, according to his theory, the body of the queen was taken from its original home and reburied, with new equipment, in either GI-a or GI-b.

Both theories, while clever, leave many details unaccounted for, such as the queen's canopic equipment, which would hardly have been left behind if her body was moved by Khufu's officials. I believe that Hetepheres was originally buried in GI-a. Lehner points out that her portable canopy and furniture would have fit almost perfectly into the burial chamber of this pyramid, which makes more sense if it was originally designed for this space. We know that a great deal of damage was done to the Giza monuments during the First Intermediate Period, a time of great upheaval in Egyptian society. I find it most likely that the queen's burial was violated during this tumultuous era, and her body taken by thieves looking for jewels and amulets. Priests loyal to the ancient royal cult might then have moved the remains of the equipment to an already existing cutting (probably dug even before Khufu came to Giza), where it remained hidden for four thousand years. This would also explain the basalt fragments found in the offering niche, which could have come from the destruction of Khufu's mortuary temple.

So, if either my theory or Mark Lehner's hypothesis is correct, one of the small pyramids, probably the northernmost one, was built for Khufu's mother, who must have lived into her son's reign and played an important role at his court. What of the other two? The southernmost pyramid (GI-c) is usually attributed to a queen named Henutsen. Her name is known to us from an inscribed slab, known as the Inventory Stele, that was found in the small temple to Isis built over the original chapel belonging to GI-c in the New Kingdom. Part of the text on this stele, which has been dated to the 18th Dynasty (c. 1500 B.C.), reads:

> Live Horus Medjedu, king of Upper and Lower Egypt, Khufu, given life. It was beside the house of the Sphinx on the northwest of the house of Osiris, lord of Rostaw, that he established the house of Isis. It was beside the temple of this goddess that he built his pyramid. It was beside this temple that he built a pyramid for the king's daughter, Henutsen.

Obviously, the writer of this text was not completely clear on his facts, since the pyramid of Khufu was built before the Sphinx. However, Henutsen is a good Old Kingdom name, and in the absence of any other attribution, we can follow the standard scholarship and hypothesize that Henutsen was one of Khufu's wives, and was buried in GI-c.

There are no texts associated with the central of the queens' pyramids (GI-b), so we must look for other information to guess who was buried there. We know the names of three other queens of Khufu: Meretyetes I, Nefertkau I, and Sedyt. Nefertkau was an "eldest daughter" of Sneferu, the mother of a prince named Neferma'at II, and the grandmother of a man named Khaf-Sneferu. We do not know for certain that she was married to Khufu, but she may have been, and thus is one

candidate for the owner of GI–b. However, a stronger possibility is Meretyetes I, who is attested in the tombs of two of her sons (one of whom,
Kawab, was an "eldest son" of Khufu). As the bearer of the titles "ornament [i.e., member of the harem] of Sneferu," "ornament of Khufu," and
"revered before Khafre," she must have held very high status in the
courts of three kings and is usually assumed to have been the daughter
of Sneferu and Hetepheres I, thus the full sister of Khufu, and most likely
his principal queen.

The Royal Children

The remainder of the eastern cemetery contains most of the largest
mastabas at Giza (except for a huge mastaba labeled G2000 in the western cemetery, whose owner is unknown). It is from these tombs that we
know the names and some of the titles (and therefore something about
the official positions within the court) of Khufu's immediate family.

One of the many things—apart from the very fragmentary nature
of the evidence—that makes determining the exact relationships between members of the royal family difficult is the vagueness of the information we are given. Among the important titles carried by many of
the people buried at Giza is *sa-nisut* (or, for a woman, *sat-nisut*). This is
generally translated as "king's son" or "king's daughter." However, as is
the case for private people who are called "son/daughter of X," the
word commonly translated as son/daughter can also mean direct de-
scendant and can occasionally refer to a grand- or great-grandchild;
later on, just to confuse things even more, the title "king's son" becomes
a ranking title that can be held by nonroyal officials. In the 4th Dynasty
distinctions are also made between *sa/sat-nisut, sa/sat-nisut en khet ef*
("king's son/daughter of his body"), and *sa/sat-nisut shemsu* ("eldest
king's son/daughter"), which can sometimes help a bit in sorting things
out. In any event, our reconstruction of the royal family must of necessity be tentative at best and factor in information from the style of the

tomb and its decoration, and from any other data we might be fortunate enough to have.

It has traditionally been assumed that the owner of the large mastaba just east of the Great Pyramid, whose name was Kawab, was the eldest son of Khufu and his principal wife, Meretyetes, and thus the crown prince. We know that he had reached middle age before he died, that he was married to Hetepheres II, who was probably his full sister, and had a daughter named Mersyankh III. The earliest known scribal statues (where a man is shown seated cross-legged on the ground, holding a papyrus in his lap) are of Kawab; these are among the very rare statues that date from Khufu's reign. It is presumed that Kawab died before Khufu and therefore never succeeded to the throne. Newer scholarship suggests that he may never have been slated to become king; he bore the title of vizier and thus must have served his father in this capacity.

Another important son was Baufre, who is known from the Westcar Papyrus (see page 46) and from a Middle Kingdom inscription in the Wadi Hammamat listing him as one of the successors of Khufu (although he is usually assumed never to have sat upon the throne of Egypt). He might have been buried in large mastaba G7310+20, whose owner is unknown. Another possibility is that he is the same prince as Baufhor, who is known from an unprovenanced granite sarcophagus now in the Cairo Museum. The only unassigned burial chamber large enough to hold this coffin is G7420; a fragment of what may well be his name survives on the wall of the chapel associated with this tomb, along with part of a title that is held only by viziers in the 4th Dynasty. The other part of this mastaba (G7410) almost certainly held the burial of a queen named Mersyankh (the second of this name, after Sneferu's mother); thus it is likely that, if G7420 was in fact his tomb, Baufhor and Mersyankh were husband and wife.

Why think that Baufhor and Baufre might be one and the same man? This is an important question and is relevant to the issue of the hypothetical new cult of Khufu. The name Baufhor, like so many Egyptian names, is compounded with the name of a god, in this case Horus; altogether, Baufhor means "His *ba* [an aspect of the soul] is Horus." Khufu's sons, for the most part, bear names compounded with either Horus or Khufu, both of which clearly refer to the king himself. If, in fact, Khufu became identified with Re, either during his lifetime or after his death, as seems very likely, perhaps the names of his sons were changed at the same time, from -hor to -re, or from -khufu to -re. This creates an interesting picture, and one that has the potential of suggesting some new (but tentative) identifications.

Tomb 7210+20 can be securely assigned to a prince (king's son of his body) named Djedefhor by virtue of the inscriptions in his tomb, although these were deliberately damaged at some point. A cult of Djedefhor had sprung up at Giza by the end of the Old Kingdom, and later tradition remembered him as a man of great wisdom, the author of some much copied "instructions," advice on how to live a good life. He is almost certainly to be identified with Prince Dedefhor of the Westcar Papyrus.

In keeping with the Baufhor/Baufre identification, it is possible, although unlikely, that Djedefhor/Dedefhor may possibly be the same man as Djedefre, Khufu's immediate successor. The question of the succession in the Old Kingdom is a difficult one; in later periods, the crown prince is clearly designated and can even serve as coregent with his father before attaining sole rule of Egypt. For the earlier periods, however, we have no way of knowing how or when the heir was appointed; we also are not certain about when people began to build, and especially to decorate, their tombs. One likely scenario for the eastern cemetery at Giza is that the mastabas were laid out but not actually assigned until potential tomb owners had reached an appropriate age and had attained the highest position within the administration they were likely to reach. We know that in some cases tomb owners advanced further up the bureaucratic ladder after parts of their tombs had been decorated, so we are fairly certain that decoration began in most cases before the owner's death.

It may have been, as is usually assumed, that the oldest son of the ruling king and his principal queen was the designated crown prince, and that the succession passed to the next eldest son if the crown prince died. This picture of events is complicated, however, by several instances in the Old Kingdom (the transition from Djedefre to Khafre, for example), when the succession passed from one brother to the next, rather than from father to son. Thus it is also possible that the succession could be open to question at the death of the king (if, for example, the king died before he could appoint a successor) or that the throne could be usurped by the strongest close relative. (There is an important myth in the Egyptian canon, told above, p. 17, that tells of the murder of Osiris by his brother, Seth, who takes the throne. Osiris's posthumous son, Horus, when he reaches his majority, challenges his uncle for the rule of Egypt and eventually succeeds in reclaiming his rightful heritage.)

In any event, it is possible that Djedefhor began his tomb while simply another prince, then abandoned it when his father died and he ascended the throne as Djedefre. Later tradition focused its memories of Djedefhor on his career as a wise adviser to his father, neglecting his short stint (probably only about eight years) as king. However, the Middle Kingdom Wadi Hammamat inscription mentioned above lists both Djedefre and Djedefhor (with an additional Re added to his name) as successors of Khufu. This would suggest that the two were separate men; in this case, the fact that there is no tomb at Giza for Djedefre might indicate that he was always intended to be the crown prince and was thus expected to build his own pyramid.

Another important son of Khufu was Khafkhufu (the first of this name). He is shown in his tomb (G7130+40) as a middle-aged man in the twenty-fourth year of Khufu's reign. His mother was an important queen, although we do not know her name. He is not given the title of vizier in his tomb; however, an architrave fragment found in one of the queens' boat pits is decorated in the same style and bears the title vizier, so it is generally assumed that Khafkhufu became vizier after his chapel was finished. Stadelmann has suggested that Khafkhufu became Khafre, the builder of the second pyramid, which seems to me to be a possibility. He may even have become a vizier during the reign of his half brother Djedefre, rather than during the reign of his father, Khufu.

Two other princes of this generation deserve mention: Khaf-Min and Neferma'at II. Khaf-Min bears the titles "eldest son of the king of his body," a title also held only by Kawab; he may be the eldest son of another of Khufu's queens. He was also a vizier, probably to Khafre, as was Neferma'at II, who was a grandson of Sneferu but not a son of Khufu.

Three daughters of Khufu are worthy of note in this discussion. Meretyetes II was buried in G7410+20, and is thought to have been the daughter of Khufu and Meretyetes I. A second possible daughter of Khufu and Meretyetes I is Hetepheres II, who seems to have been married three times: to Kawab, Ankhhaf, and Djedefre. She was buried with her first husband, Kawab, and is mentioned in the tomb of her daughter, Mersyankh III. A new name appears during this generation, that of Khamerernebty; she was a daughter of Khufu and an unnamed queen, and married to Khafre.

To summarize: Khufu's principal wife was Meretyetes I, who may have borne him five children (Kawab, Baufhor/Baufre, Djedefhor, Djedefre, Merytyetes II, and Hetepheres II). Henutsen was possibly the mother of Khafkhufu/Khafre and Khaf-Min. Sneferu's daughter Nefertkau I may have been the mother of Neferma'at II and a wife of Khafkhufu's named Nefertkau II. Of the last queen, we have only a name, Sedyt.

Khufu's Administration

It seems that most, if not all, of Khufu's sons eventually gained the title of vizier, although not all of them held the title during their father's reign. In addition, we know of at least two other viziers belonging to Khufu's generation. Hemiunu, assumed to be Khufu's first and most important adviser, was buried in tomb G4000 in the western cemetery (finished in the nineteenth year of Khufu's reign); this important man was the son of Sneferu's vizier Neferma'at I and was thus either Khufu's cousin or his nephew. Ankhhaf was a king's eldest son, perhaps of Sneferu and a minor wife, and was buried in one of the large mastabas in the eastern field, G7510, and was thus a member of Khufu's immediate family. It is difficult to reconstruct exactly who lived when and who might have served as Khufu's vizier during which part of his reign.

Various scholars have drawn up differing sequences for these viziers. With a certain number of viziers to fit into a limited period of time, it is often assumed that princes were advanced to this post only after ascending the ranks slowly, at which point they were relatively old and likely to die rather soon. Another possibility, not commonly mentioned, is that more than one vizier could serve at a time, which is certainly the case in the New Kingdom, when there were usually two viziers serving simultaneously.

Regardless of who acted as vizier when during the reign of Khufu, it seems that this all-important bureaucrat was ultimately responsible, below the king, for all aspects of the central administration, with duties in all domains. Below the vizier were many layers of bureaucracy. In contrast to the sort of specialization we see today, especially in Western nations, ancient Egyptian officials could have duties, apparently simultaneously, in different aspects of the administration.

One important branch of the administration was the military, responsible for conducting foreign expeditions and for securing the right to the mines where the raw materials needed to build the pyramid (as well as materials for luxury goods) were found. The military was organized in a tribal fashion, with units coming from around the country but centralized at the capital and headed by a royal official. The duty of the army was to maintain peace within the borders of Egypt and to protect expeditions to foreign lands.

Taxes collected from around the country, including the capital, flowed into the royal treasury, which was itself divided into two branches, one for Upper Egypt and the other for Lower Egypt. The royal treasure houses stored gold, silver, grain, and other valuable items. Both departments were under the supervision of one person, a treasurer of Upper and Lower Egypt, who was responsible for all the records. Egypt was divided into regions known as nomes. The rulers of these nomes were appointed by the king. In lieu of paying taxes, the nomarchs probably sent workers and supplies directly to the pyramid project.

The fact that this extraordinary project could be carried out attests to the excellent administration that functioned under Khufu. The key seems to have been many small departments that were then amalgamated into larger departments overseen by a single official. There was a department responsible only for the exploration of the mines and quarries of Egypt and Sinai. The department of public service oversaw the transport of materials and people. The department of public works was responsible for the planning and construction of the palace, the tombs, and the canals and lakes connected with irrigation. Local irrigation was controlled by the nomarchs. Trade to the south, where ivory, ostrich eggs, wood, leather, and gold were found, was supervised by the governors of Aswan. Other trade went north and east, to Syria and Lebanon, for coniferous woods and olive oil. But all these departments were overseen by high royal officials, who in turn answered to the vizier and then to the king.

Most of the officials of Khufu's administration who did not belong to his immediate family or direct line of descent were buried, like Hemiunu, in the western cemetery. This necropolis is bounded on the south by a massive limestone wall running from east to west. It is built of huge rocks, and runs across Khufu's old quarry. A fieldstone enclosure wall bounds the cemetery on the east. Within these limits, four nucleus cemeteries of stone tombs were arranged in streets and avenues. These were designated by their excavators as cemeteries G1200, G2100, G4000, and the cemetery *en echelon*. By the twentieth year of Khufu's reign, the royal builders had completed the core mastabas in cemetery G4000, arranged east-southeast of the tomb of Hemiunu (tomb G4000 itself).

Khufu's necropolis planners left a space 140 to 150 meters (459 to 492 feet) wide between the Great Pyramid and cemeteries G4000 and 12000, presumably either to allow passage of the great ramps and embankments necessary for the building of the pyramid or for galleries similar to those west of Khafre's pyramid, which were used as workshops and storage areas.

The largest tomb at Giza was G2000 in the western cemetery; inside it was found the skeleton of an old man, but no inscriptions remained in the tomb, whose chapel had been razed to the ground. We know that this man must have been extremely important in the administration, but we know nothing about him, not even his name.

The superstructures of the first tombs built in this cemetery contained simple niches at the southern end of the east side. Within these niches were emplacements for small slab steles of fine limestone carved in relief and then painted with images of the tomb owners, identified by their names and titles, seated before tables heaped with offerings. One of the most beautiful of these was carved for a man name Wepemnofret, who sits on a stool supported by carved bulls' legs before his table of plenty. These small offering niches, fronted by mud-brick chapels, represent a peculiar regression from the decorated chapels, filled with scenes from everyday life, found in tombs from the reign of Sneferu. Late in the reign of Khufu, the decoration of private tombs became more elaborate again, perhaps because work on Khufu's pyramid and temples was nearing completion. The old mastabas were remodeled, their mud-brick chapels pulled down, and small, stepped stone mastabas were erected, encased in retaining walls built of great blocks of fine white limestone. Interior L-shaped chapels were built into these remodeled mastabas, their stone-lined walls decorated with carved and painted reliefs. The original slab steles were sealed behind the new stonework.

A number of the Giza tombs contain reserve heads. Of the thirty-seven of these found to date (mostly at Giza), a number were discovered at the bottom of the burial shafts, rather than in the chapel or burial chamber as might have been expected. Each head has unique, almost idiosyncratic features, but at the same time, the features are clearly idealized in their simplicity, and their expressions are beatific gazes toward the beyond. Some have crude incisions down the back of the head and similarly rude breaks around the ears. None bears an inscription, and their function is still a matter of scholarly debate. They have been variously identified as sculptor's models, extra images of the tomb owner in case the body is lost, or even wig stands.

Chapter Ten

The Completion of the Great Pyramid and the Death of Khufu

In the thirtieth year of his reign, Khufu began to feel the aches and pains of age and infirmity, and he knew that his death would be coming soon. But he didn't mind so much: the country was safe and secure, and he knew his cult would be maintained. His pyramid was finished, awaiting his burial and resurrection, and he had taken to going inside, into the chamber into which his sarcophagus was set, to find the quiet out of which his best thoughts would come. Before he left this world to fly to the sky to join his fellow gods, he was determined to finish writing his sacred book and leave a legacy for his descendants, so he would have his servants bring his scribal equipment and papyrus scroll, then leave him in peace for hours at a time.

We do not know the contents of Khufu's sacred book, for which he was remembered by later generations, but we can guess that it might have held the knowledge that he had gained over the course of his life, perhaps the science he had learned through the building of his pyramid, or the religious epiphanies that had led to his change of cult. It may have told the story of a conspiracy or have contained advice for his sons and successors. Copies of this book have never been found, but if any existed, the most likely place to look for them would be inside the pyramid itself.

Once the pyramid was completed, the spiral ramp that hid the face of the monumental benben would then have been dismantled and deposited in the quarry from which the core stones had been taken. As the workers descended, they would have smoothed and cleaned the fine limestone casing that had been put in place as the pyramid rose. Once the ramps had been removed, the two southern boat pits were cut, and Khufu's small cult pyramid was erected near the southeast corner of the main pyramid.

From reliefs found in association with other pyramids, we know that the installation of the capstone, also known as the pyramidion, was a very important event, a joyous celebration for all Egypt. Unless this ceremony occurred before the ramp was dismantled, it is likely that the architects left a section of the ramp against one face of the pyramid, probably the north, so that the capstone could be put in place. It would not have been an easy feat, as the builders would have been working in very confined quarters, and the stone itself would have been very heavy. The capstone would have been carved of a special stone quarried in the Egyptian deserts, under hazardous conditions, and then cased by the royal workshop with gold that would gleam in the sun.

It is tempting to imagine that Khufu might have combined his Sed festival, which served in part to mark the completion of all that the gods had asked the king to do—building his tomb, along with temples for his worship as a god and for the worship of Horus, Hathor, and Re; smiting the enemies of Egypt and keeping them at bay; and doing what was necessary to keep the country wealthy, stable, and prosperous—with the dedication of his pyramid.

Let us imagine the events that might have taken place on this momentous day:

An announcement had been made in every nome of Egypt, from the Great Green (the Mediterranean Sea) to Aswan. Those who could came to the capital; others celebrated in their hometowns. But all joined in the rejoicing. Flags were hung in temples all over Egypt. The boats that plied the Nile were decorated with flowers. Everyone in the country had new clothes to wear. Music was practiced in every village, and ritual dances were rehearsed. Each of the over one million Egyptians prepared for the big day.

On the morning of the celebration, Khufu arose early. His servants prepared his bath and breakfast and readied his robe and crowns. When he left his palace, he was accompanied by his immediate family and by the royal musical troupe. He was met by his vizier in the north court of the pyramid, and together they examined the capstone that was to crown the great monument. The specially trained workmen began to ascend the face of the pyramid, with music playing and dancers dancing; when they reached the top, Khufu gave the sign for them to set the golden pyramidion in place.

Wearing his enveloping Sed robe and the double crown of the Two Lands, Khufu entered the subterranean chamber of his small ritual pyramid. Alone inside, he removed the crowns and the robe, and reemerged into the light of day wearing a kilt and holding the royal flail. Striding boldly out of the pyramid and into the main pyramid court, he performed the ritual dance that proved his strength, vitality, and virility (despite his age), and announced that he had become the universal god

of Egypt and had only to wait for the moment when he would die so he could

travel to heaven and join the stars. He was watched by his queens, children, and

highest officials; the rest of the nobles and the general public were not permitted

inside the complex and could not observe this ritual, but they could join in the

festivities that accompanied it.

When Khufu finished the dance, a shout went up from the crowd. The king

once again entered the chamber of his small pyramid and reemerged wearing the

robe and crown and carrying the flail. Those fortunate enough to be a part of the

inner circle accompanied him back out of the complex, where he appeared in glory

to his loyal subjects, and then to his palace, where the feasting began.

Final Clues: The Burial of Khufu

It was long believed that Khufu ruled for twenty-three years, as is recorded in the New Kingdom Turin Canon (a document listing all the kings of Egypt and the lengths of their reigns, at least as they were remembered at that point). However, a newly discovered inscription found in the Dakhla Oasis in the western desert records an expedition sent by Khufu in the twenty-seventh year of his reign. As we know, the early kings of Egypt often numbered their reigns according to the biennial cattle count, so the Turin Canon may have confused a count of twenty-three with a reign of twenty-three years. If the New Kingdom recorders had access to a count of twenty-three, then Khufu might have reigned for as many as forty-six years. Another possibility is that the Turin recorder just gave each Giza king approximately a generation in which to rule. My best estimate, based on the available evidence, is that Khufu ruled for thirty to thirty-two years, and may have been fifty-eight or sixty when he died.

Khufu's funeral would have been supervised by his successor, in this case Djedefre, who left his cartouche on the slabs covering the boat pits south of the pyramid. He would have been aided by Khufu's vizier, perhaps Ankhhaf, as Hemiunu may already have died. The body of the king would first have been taken to his valley temple and laid on a bed beneath a purification tent, a temporary structure erected for the performance of the purification rites. After the proper rituals had been performed, the body would have been taken to the embalming workshop, where it would stay for forty days immersed in natron to remove the moisture and another thirty days to complete the process of mummification.

On the day of the funeral, the royal mummy was placed inside a golden coffin, which was carried to the north side of the pyramid by a procession of priests. Once the coffin reached the pyramid entrance, Ankhhaf halted the procession and dismissed all but two of the priests. Leaving the other mourners behind, he led the coffin bearers through the entrance chamber to the central of the three chambers. An open area had been left behind one wall, and the priests slid the coffin into this secret chamber and sealed the room completely. When Ankhhaf emerged with the two priests, he ordered that the pyramid entrance be sealed, protecting the secret knowledge that Khufu was not, after all, buried in the chamber with the granite sarcophagus but was hidden where he would remain safe for eternity. Even the next king, Djedefre, did not know the secret.

Part Three

The Heirs
of Khufu

Chapter Eleven

Battles Stir Within the Royal Family

Djedefre at Abu Rawash

The days before the death of Khufu, when the once-powerful king lay helpless on his sickbed, were filled with turmoil in the royal family. And then he died, and the passing of the god was announced to the land. Grief blanketed the country, and within the palace there were whispers and rumors. Would Djedefre succeed, or would his half brother Khafre take the throne from him? But Djedefre was the elder, the official crown prince, and had influence within the royal council. And so he won the battle and took over preparations for his father's burial. He asked the chief carpenter, Intyshedu, to finish the dismantling of two great wooden boats that were to be placed inside the two boat pits south of his father's pyramid. As evidence for his role in his father's burial, he had his name, newly enclosed inside the royal cartouche, inscribed eighteen times on the slabs that sealed these pits.

When he ascended the throne of the Two Lands, Djedefre took on a new epithet, "son of Re," as a tribute to the cult of his father. He adopted three additional names: the Horus Kheper ("the one who exists"); the

Two Ladies Kheperemnebty; and the Horus of Gold (with three falcons).

After he had buried his father, Djedefre left Giza and the intrigues of his brother Khafre, moving his court to Abu Rawash, eight kilometers (five miles) to the north. He was already married, to a princess named Khentetenka, but to ensure his claim to the throne, he also married his brother Kawab's widow, Hetepheres II. We do not know the name of the architect who planned his pyramid complex, but we know that it was called "Djedefre is a *sehed*-star."

From its vantage point on a high hillock, one hundred fifty meters (492 feet) above the Nile Valley, Djedefre's pyramid overlooks the Giza plateau. The mound that stood there already provided a core for the pyramid, saving enormous amounts of effort. The pyramid itself was planned as a relatively modest structure with steep sides, comparable to the original slope of the southern pyramid of his grandfather Sneferu at Dahshur. It is usually assumed that Djedefre did not have access to the resources commanded by his father and later by his brother Khafre; it is equally possible that he was fairly advanced in age when he came to the throne (we know that his children were already grown) and knew that he might not have time to finish a more ambitious project.

The core of the pyramid (of which only a fraction remains today) consists partly of the reshaped rocky subsoil and partly of blocks of limestone; there is also evidence on the eastern side that the pyramid was cased in granite. The recent discovery of a copper ax blade buried at the site demonstrates that a foundation ceremony was carried out. The substructure of the pyramid is about twenty-three meters by ten meters (seventy-six feet by thirty-three feet) and reaches a depth below the surface of about twenty meters (sixty-six feet). The access corridor is about forty-nine meters (161 feet) long. Two rooms were planned, one as a burial chamber and the other as a *serdab*. In 1880, Petrie found some pieces of granite in the substructure, and some scholars believe that these were pieces of the royal sarcophagus.

To the east of the pyramid are remains of a hastily built mortuary temple, constructed of fieldstone finished with mud brick. In this area, the name of Djedefre, written within a cartouche, was found, along with part of a pillar. A boat pit, shaped with hull and prow, was found on the south side of this temple, filled with statue fragments made of reddish quartzite. There were about one hundred and twenty statues smashed and thrown into this pit. The fragments come from statues representing the king seated on his throne, his queens, and three of his sons and two of his daughters. One of the most extraordinary fragments is a beautiful quartzite head of the king himself. This is the head of a sphinx, the first example known of this magical creature. The Egyptian sphinx has the body of a lion and the head of a king, and it symbolizes the might and power of the Egyptian monarch. The way in which these statues were destroyed looks more like revenge than simple vandalism. Some scholars take this as evidence of internecine fighting between Djedefre and Khafre; it is also possible that this destruction was carried out later, during the First Intermediate Period, when Giza itself was vandalized, or during the Roman period, or even more recently, when people came to the site to take away stones for modern building projects.

At the southwest corner of the main pyramid is evidence of a cult pyramid. Recent excavations by a joint project of the Swiss and the SCA found a new pyramid near the southeast corner of the main pyramid. The base is about 10.5 meters (thirty-four feet), and five courses of limestone still stand on each side. In the middle of the north side of this pyramid was a shaft, one and a half meters (five feet) square and about four meters (thirteen feet) deep, which led to a north-south passage off which were three rooms, one to the east and two to the west. Inside the shaft were shards of Old Kingdom pottery and vessels from the Roman period. In addition, some remarkable artifacts were found here, including a piece of mortar in the shape of the type of mat found under Djoser's southern tomb. In the main passage was a large alabaster bowl bearing the Horus name of Khufu; a basalt weight inscribed with the weight of

90 deben, the equivalent of about 810 grams (about two pounds); a bread mold; and two canopic jars. These jars are the earliest known examples of such vessels. The eastern room contained pieces of a sarcophagus lid.

This pyramid clearly belonged to a queen, perhaps Queen Hetepheres II. The location of this pyramid is in the spot usually reserved for the ritual pyramid, but many aspects of Djedefre's complex differ from the layout used by his father and followed by later kings. In fact, it is laid out more like the earlier complex of Djoser, as if this king chose to ally himself with the more distant past.

The other pyramid found might have been for Queen Khentetenka; many fragments of statues belonging to this queen have been found at Abu Rawash.

Work on Djedefre's pyramid proceeded rapidly during his reign, but without the high standards conformed to by the builders of Khufu's pyramid. It is generally believed that Djedefre ruled for only eight years; when he died, his pyramid complex was left in its unfinished state. There is no evidence that his successor, his brother Khafre, tried to finish the pyramid. However, one statue fragment, of a throne, so probably of a seated king, bears the inscription "Men . . . re" (Menkaure); thus it is possible that this later king did some work on this pyramid.

Djedefre's pyramid is approached by a very long causeway that joins the enclosure wall of the pyramid on its northern side. A covered corridor links the inner enclosure that surrounds the mortuary temple with this causeway; a cache of small offering vessels was found just outside this corridor. This pottery suggests that the cult service for Djedefre continued for a significant period; that, despite the unfinished condition of his complex, he was not abandoned after his death.

We know little of the character of Djedefre. The sphinx head, now in the Louvre, depicts him as a wise man, a profound thinker, and a firm man. His sons are shown as scribes (some of the earliest scribal statues known), telling us that they were educated and trusted by their father. If he was indeed the same man as Djedefhor, he was remembered as a wise man, the author of some important didactic literature.

Due to the destruction wreaked on his complex, we have very little evidence for his reign. We also know nothing about the circumstances surrounding his death. The theorists who believe that the royal sons of Khufu fought over his throne might suggest that Djedefre had killed his brother Kawab, and that Khafre took revenge by killing Djedefre. Perhaps, they would say, Djedefre's pyramid complex was left unfinished and his statues destroyed out of hatred and the desire that his name and cult be lost forever. But we know that his cult did continue: in addition to the cache of votive pottery found at Abu Rawash, there are priests of Djedefre buried at Giza, and there were donation decrees and records of offerings made to his cult by the descendants of Khafre.

Chapter Twelve

The Conspiracies of Khafre

His half brother Djedefre had succeeded in taking the throne of Egypt. But now Djedefre was dead, and it was his turn. None of Djedefre's sons were strong enough to defeat him. He had the support of his father's advisers; and Khafre, still young enough to look forward to a significant reign, knew that this time he would triumph, that now it was his chance to sit upon the Egyptian throne and guide the Two Lands. Younger than his brothers, he had been his father's favorite, and they had spent many hours together discussing the ways of ma'at: how best to rule the land, and how to follow the will of the gods in the sky while playing the role of god on earth. They had read the ancient manuscripts together and argued fine points of theology and dogma. Khafre had always known that he was his father's proper successor, and now the moment he had long awaited would come to pass.

Prince Khafkhufu, who we believe might well be the same man as Khafre, is depicted as middle-aged in his mastaba to the east of the Great Pyramid; a quarry mark from the tomb suggests that the tomb was being built in the twenty-fourth year of Khufu's reign. He was a king's son of his body, and most likely a son of Khufu; his mother was certainly a queen, perhaps Henutsen, the queen buried in the southernmost of the small queens' pyramids. His wife was Nefertkau, and he had at least two sons and one daughter.

If Khafkhufu and Khafre are the same, he may have married his half sister Mersyankh II, daughter of Khufu and Meretyetes.

Khafre's first move as king was to bring the court back to Giza. There is no evidence that a new palace was built for him here; therefore, I believe that he took over his father's palace, probably repainting it with new scenes to celebrate his own reign.

His first vizier was Ankhhaf, who bore the title of overseer of all the king's works. This man was buried in tomb G7510, the second largest tomb at Giza. Some scholars believe that he was the son of Sneferu; others think that he was the son of Khufu and the brother of Khafre. This is the man who would have announced the appearance of the new king to the forty-two nomes of Upper and Lower Egypt. Perhaps the priests of Heliopolis were less than thrilled by the return to Giza and the ideology of Khufu, which may have been less prominent during the reign of Djedefre.

We can imagine that Khafre took the throne during the season of *peret*, when the crops grew. By the season of *shemu*, harvest, the move to Giza would have been completed and the court settled into the houses they had left only twelve years before, welcomed back by the priests and administrators who had stayed behind to tend to the cult of Khufu. During the four months of *shemu*, the new king's architects and engineers began to survey the site for his pyramid, which was to be almost as large as his father's. To the south and west of the Great Pyramid, they found a suitable spot, on a rise that would put Khafre's new monument slightly higher than its predecessor.

Preparations for the new pyramid might have stretched on into *akhet*, the flood season that began the agricultural cycle of the year. A high flood could be dangerous; a low flood could leave the fields with too little water for a good crop yield and make it hard to bring supplies and stones to the pyramid site. A good flood meant a good year ahead, and was an important omen for the future.

While the site was prepared, Khafre and his advisers would have been choosing a name for the new pyramid. This was extremely important, identifying the powerful symbol of the pyramid, the point where life and death, light and darkness, met and were transformed. Khufu had chosen Akhet Khufu, which meant "horizon of Khufu," but also incorporated the meaning of transformation, of emerging from the darkness to shine in glory. Khafre chose to name his pyramid Khafre Wer ("Khafre is great").

A New Kingdom stele found close to the lower temple near the site of the rest house of Tutankhamen reads: "A gift the king gives to Anubis, who is on his mountain, that he might give to the chief of the pyramid city, 'Khafre is great.' " This tells us that there was a pyramid city of Khafre distinct from the pyramid city of Khufu and that the name of the city was, as usual, the same as the name of the pyramid. The exact location of this settlement was most likely in front of the east facade of the lower temple, east of the terrace and the canal that ran in front of it. We also know from titles borne by courtiers buried at Giza that at least one area of Khafre's pyramid city was called Ten-resy. Thus scholars believe that the pyramid city of Khafre was located south of his causeway and lower temple.

It is in this city that Khafre's administration and priesthood would have lived. The workers, artisans, and minor officials involved in the construction of his pyramid were housed farther to the south, in the area near the Wall of the Crow. All these men and women would have been working together, serving their new king and ensuring Egypt's position on earth and Khafre's future as a god.

Chapter Thirteen

The Pyramid Complex of Khafre

Khafre, the new king, was not young, but he was healthy and virile, and determined to match his father. His pyramid would be almost as large, and he would make certain that its complex was properly laid out and beautifully decorated. His brother's sculptors had come back to Giza with them, and the practice they had gotten at Abu Rawash would serve him well. He would order many statues of himself, all perfectly carved in hard, gleaming stone. His image would grace his temples, and ensure that his ka would never want for an eternal home.

*T*he pyramid complex of Khafre is very well preserved. Its layout can still be seen clearly, and its temples and causeway are the most visited of any pyramid complex. In its basics, it follows the plan set out by the complex of Khufu. It is entered from the east through a valley temple, which is still standing to much of its original height. Recent work has revealed evidence for a large harbor that lay in front of this temple. Nineteen meters (sixty-two feet) to the east of the temple, Old Kingdom remains lie just below the surface. In 1980, Mark Lehner and I opened a trench only fourteen meters (forty-six feet) farther to the east and found pure sand stretching to the bedrock six meters (twenty feet) below surface level. Another eighteen meters (fifty-nine feet) to the east of our trench, the Ministry of Irrigation, as part of our Sphinx Conservation Project, drilled to find the level of the water table. Their drills went through about fifteen meters (forty-nine feet) of sand and water-soaked debris before hitting hard surface, indicating a steep drop-off and confirming the presence of an ancient harbor, the pyramid harbor of Khafre, in this location. The core drills also pulled up fragments of red granite imported from Aswan. This granite almost certainly comes from Khafre's valley temple, either fallen there during construction or thrown from the ancient monuments during a later period.

This harbor would have been the place in which boats from up and down the Nile docked to deliver their loads of grain, cattle, or stone to support the royal pyramid project. From the harbor, the boats would have unloaded their goods onto a landing stage in front of the valley temple. In 1996, as a part of the site management program, we removed a modern cement stage in front of the valley temple that had been used in the past for shows by entertainers such as Frank Sinatra, Billy Pearl, and even the Grateful Dead. When we removed the stage, we found some curious structures in the area just east of the temple.

The temple itself has two entrances set on a platform that runs the length of its facade. The northern entrance is for the goddess Bastet and the southern one is for Hathor. These two entrances to the temple represent the duality of the north and south and underline the function of the king as lord of the Two Lands. Leading to these entrances are two limestone paths, ending in the east in two ramps sloping down, probably to the as-yet uncovered harbor quay. The ramps are more than twenty-four meters (seventy-nine feet) long and from 1.2 to 1.5 meters (four to five feet) wide. Cut emplacements and arcs worn into the surface of the stone provide evidence for wooden doors that once closed now-vanished entrance kiosks.

Beneath each ramp is a sort of trench or tunnel cut into the bedrock. Parallel mud-brick walls between the tunnels and to their north and south formed a corridor about 4 meters (thirteen feet) wide. Evidence from the New Kingdom indicates that the king, both symbolically and actually, needed boats to control the Two Lands, and I believe that these tunnels were for the sacred boat for the king as Horus, used to help him watch over the north and south of Egypt. Mark Lehner sees these tunnels as reservoirs, token bodies of water that people approaching the valley temple via these ramps would cross over as they passed through the kiosks into the sacred space. They may also simply be passageways so that workers or other people not authorized to enter the sacred pyramid precincts could pass from south to north without having to go around the entire complex.

The terrace fronting the temple itself is about 6.7 meters (twenty-two feet) from east to west. On this surface, our recent excavations have revealed emplacements for four large sphinxes, two flanking each doorway, and traces of the purification tent in which the body of the king would have been placed on a bed and washed. A mud-brick platform to the northeast might have served as a viewing area for the royal family. The water from the washing would have been saved, as it was considered sacred.

The valley temple was once surrounded on three sides by an enclosure wall of limestone blocks, of which the southern part still exists. The core of the temple is made of limestone blocks that were then cased with pink granite from Aswan. There is evidence found in niches high up on the back walls for statues of oversized baboons, who would have been shown standing to greet the rising sun. The floor was paved with gleaming yellow alabaster, to emphasize Khafre's connection with the sun god.

The walls were not decorated; instead, sockets for twenty-three or twenty-four statues of the king, which would have substituted for the program of wall reliefs seen in Khufu's temple, line the interior of the T-shaped main chamber. Fragments of several of these statues were found by Auguste Mariette, first director of the Egyptian Antiquities Department, inside an irregular pit in the northern part of the vestibule of the temple, where they had been hidden at some point in antiquity. (Tourists now throw money into this pit for good luck, and the guards collect it each week to use to pay for the protection of the monuments.) The most famous of these statues is one of the greatest masterpieces of the Cairo Museum: it shows Khafre, wearing a kilt and the nemes head-dress, seated on a high-backed throne on which the Horus falcon perches and spreads his wings to embrace the head of the king. The statue identifies Khafre with Horus and simultaneously places him under the protection of this god. Seen from the side, it looks as if Horus will take the king with him and fly to the sky. On another level, the statue represents the divine triad of Isis, Osiris, and Horus: the throne is the hieroglyphic sign for the name of Isis; the king himself is Osiris; and the hawk behind him is Horus. The statue is made of diorite, a hard stone quarried far to the south in the deserts of Nubia; the artisan who carved it breathed such life into it that the royal blood seems to flow beneath the skin.

The temple was roofed but left with holes on the top to bring the rays of sun inside the temple and reflect off the alabaster. In addition to the main chamber, there are storage rooms spanning two stories.

There is a corridor running from the T-shaped main chamber to the causeway, which can thus be entered directly from the valley temple. The causeway runs west for about a quarter of a mile; the walls were cased with fine limestone, but there is no evidence that they were ever decorated. It ends at the mortuary temple in front of the pyramid itself. Inside this structure, perhaps the largest Old Kingdom temple known, were many statues of the king.

This temple is built of blocks of locally quarried limestone that can weigh up to two hundred tons apiece. The layout of the temple echoes the standard style of the Old Kingdom, with an entrance hall, a court, five statue niches, offering rooms, and magazines. The Egyptians had names for each part of the temple: the vestibule was called the *per-weru* ("place of the great ones"), the court was called *uskhet* ("wide"), and the sanctuary was called *tepkhet* ("caverns"). In the open court of this temple was a huge table on which the people would have placed their offerings. The five statue niches contained images of the king and gods. Three niches contained images of Khafre as a god, one of the goddess Hathor, and I believe that the fifth niche might have contained a statue of Khufu as the god Re. The sanctuary, into which no one but the king and the priests could enter, lay to the west of the court, and at the pyramid base is an offering area that may once have consisted of an altar and two steles.

The pyramid itself was surrounded by an enclosure wall and a pyramid court. Like Khufu's pyramid, Khafre's monument was built of locally quarried limestone and cased with fine limestone from Tura, some of which still clings to the upper part of the pyramid. In contrast to Khufu, who used only limestone on the exterior of his pyramid, Khafre cased the lowest course with granite. The pyramid of Khafre retains most of its top (although the capstone is gone). A slight twist at the top tells us that Khafre's engineers were not quite as skilled as his father's—the orientation of the pyramid had gotten off track, and the architects had to compensate for this error.

There are two entrance passages leading to the interior chambers of the pyramid, suggesting that there was a change in plan at one point that modified the size or position of the pyramid base. One passage begins in the body of the pyramid, about eleven and a half meters (thirty-eight feet) above the level of the base behind the north face, and descends to just below ground level, to a horizontal corridor that runs to the burial chamber. The other begins at ground level in front of the north baseline, descends to a horizontal corridor, then ascends to join with the horizontal corridor that leads to the burial chamber. Along the horizontal corridor accessed from the second entrance is a rectangular chamber whose purpose is unclear; it may have been a *serdab* for the statue of the king.

The burial chamber lies east of the midpoint of the pyramid. Near the west wall of this chamber, a black granite sarcophagus closed by a sliding lid is embedded in the floor; holes in the underside of the lid probably held copper pins that dropped into corresponding holes in the coffin when it was in place. When this chamber was first entered in 1818 (by an Italian circus performer turned archaeologist named Giovanni Belzoni), the bones of a bull were found inside the sarcophagus. A rectangular pit seventy-six centimeters (thirty inches) long, seventy-two centimeters (twenty-eight inches) wide, and seventy centimeters (twenty-seven inches) deep, is cut into the floor of the chamber; this must have contained the canopic chest that once held the royal viscera. Although Khafre's interior chambers are not as impressive as those of Khufu, they have their own magnificence and style. The upper descending passage is lined with granite, and the whole system has an air of simplicity and elegance.

It is very important to note that the chambers inside the pyramid are underground, in stark contrast to the chambers in the pyramid of Khufu. They were probably built inside a pit, as had been done by Djedefre at Abu Rawash. The simple construction of the corridor and the burial chamber suggests that the builders tried to avoid the problems faced by the builders of Khufu's pyramid. It is unlikely that the real burial chamber of Khafre is hidden somewhere inside the pyramid. Although many expeditions have used X-rays and radar to search for hidden rooms, and some have found indications of hollow areas, the interior masonry is not laid regularly and includes gaps and spaces. However, it is tempting to speculate that the Giza kings were cleverer than all of us and managed to hide their burials from the tomb robbers who soon invaded their sacred monuments, leaving the obvious burial chambers behind as red herrings. Perhaps one day we will develop new and better techniques for noninvasive exploration and learn the true story.

On the south side of Khafre's pyramid were found the remains of what is either a satellite pyramid or a queen's pyramid. In 1960, four meters (thirteen feet) to the west of this pyramid and aligned with its east-west center axis, Abdel Hafez Abd el-Al found a sealed passage, eighty centimeters (thirty-one inches) in cross-section, that slopes downward for a total length of 7.15 meters (twenty-three feet). At the end on the south side was found a small niche 1.19 meters (four feet) long. Inside the niche was a wooden box sealed with string that contained three layers of wooden pieces that have been reconstructed as a frame of four rods supporting a cavetto cornice. Some Old Kingdom tomb scenes show funerary statues being dragged on sledges encased in tall rectangular shrines of this form. The proximity of the passage to the subsidiary pyramid indicates that the passage was an annex to the pyramid substructure; the burial of a statue shrine in this passage suggests that a statue was transported to the subsidiary pyramid and placed in its burial chamber. There is no evidence that this pyramid was used for a burial, so it is usually assumed that it was a cult, rather than a queen's, pyramid.

There is an area of narrow galleries (more than one hundred of them!) directly west of Khafre's pyramid, known as the workmen's barracks, the name assigned to it by its first excavator, W. M. F. Petrie. Recent clearance of this area proved that this is a misnomer, that the area was instead used for the storage of goods needed for the funerary cult; it was also used as a workshop in which items for the cult were manufactured.

Scholars are still arguing about the function of the pyramid complex as a whole, and about the function of its individual elements; for the 4th Dynasty, Khafre's complex is the best preserved, and thus is used as evidence for various theories. Some scholars have argued that the purpose of the pyramid complex was to provide an appropriate setting for the funeral of the king. Certain Egyptologists have identified holes on the top of Khafre's valley temple, which they interpret as emplacements for a tent, as evidence that the purification ceremonies for the body of the king took place here and that the actual mummification took place inside the temple itself. After the body had been mummified, the chief priest, who was also the crown prince, with the aid of other priests, would have laid the mummy inside its coffin and led the funeral procession through the causeway to the upper temple. In this temple, they would have recited prayers and performed the proper rituals, then passed through the temple to the pyramid court and thence into the pyramid itself, where the body of the king would be laid to rest forever.

However, the scenes decorating the temples and causeways of other complexes do not include depictions of the funeral; thus it is very unlikely that this was its primary purpose. On a very practical note, the door that connects the funerary temple with the pyramid court is too narrow to permit passage of a funeral procession. In addition, our new excavations in front of the valley temple have ascertained that the purification of the king's body was done on the platform outside the valley temple and that the mummification was done inside a workshop that lay to the south.

Other scholars have suggested that the valley temple was used by the king as a rest house when he visited the building site of his pyramid. However, since we now know that the king lived in a palace at the foot of the plateau, this theory is no longer valid. Another idea is that the valley temple was used for feasts. According to this hypothesis, the people, led by priests, would greet the statues inside the temple and make offerings. Prayers would be recited and music played; the priests would bless the people, who would then leave via the back door, enter the causeway, and walk the half kilometer (0.3 miles) to the funerary temple. But we are certain that access to the complex was extremely restricted, and that only priests were permitted inside, so this theory is less than compelling.

Careful analysis of the architecture of the 4th Dynasty complexes, in conjunction with what we know about their decoration and information from textual sources, tells us that the monuments functioned as important centers of worship, dedicated to the cult of kingship. The complex was a sacred space, within which the king in his guise as Horus carried out his proper duties (such as defeating the enemies of Egypt and performing the rites of the Sed festival), and was in turn rewarded with the kingship itself and granted identification with the king of the gods, the sun god Re. There is even a progression within the complex: the king's role as Horus is most explicit in the valley temple and causeway, and he is worshipped as Re within the upper temple. The queen had an important role to play also; as we have seen, she was an incarnation of Hathor, daughter of Re and wife of Horus. The complex thus was an architectural expression of ancient Egyptian religious dogma, made eternal in stone.

The Great Sphinx

A unique feature of Khafre's pyramid complex is the Great Sphinx. This colossal sculpture, with the elongated body of a lion and the head of a king, lies at the eastern edge of the plateau, guarding the entrance to the sacred space where Khafre and his father, and later his son, were buried. It was carved out of the living rock of the plateau, and includes three different strata of limestone. The newly invented solar symbol of the sphinx, first seen during the reign of Djedefre, was a powerful image of the king blended with the strength and power of a lion. Between twenty and thirty times life size, the Great Sphinx also represents the first colossal statue preserved to us from ancient Egypt.

In 1988, we began a conservation program designed to restore parts of the Sphinx that were falling apart and preserve it for future generations. When we initiated this project, the rock of the Sphinx's body was badly deteriorated, although the head is in much better shape. We included two well-known sculptors in our Sphinx conservation plan, so that we could, for the first time, attempt to understand the modeling of the Sphinx. We can now appreciate the enormous skill possessed by the ancient artists, and have a better idea of the techniques they used to work with the soft stone.

In order to carve the Sphinx, the quarrymen would first have removed the surrounding bedrock in a U-shape, creating a ditch and leaving the rock core, which would become the statue standing in the center. The Sphinx's body is composed mostly of poor-quality layers of mother rock (labeled Member II by geologists) with many vertical fissures. This stratum of weak rock weathers very easily and comes away in flakes and powder. At the lowest level of the Sphinx, making up the lowest part of the lion's body and the base, there is a harder stratum of stone. This does not weather easily, but it is very rough and brittle (Member I). There are some large fissures in the body of the Sphinx that pass through Member II and right down into Member I. Since the natural limestone was formed long before the Egyptians arrived at Giza, the Sphinx's body layers were, of course, already of poor quality in the Old Kingdom.

The stratum from which the Sphinx's face, beard, head, and neck were carved (Member III) is a much harder, better-quality limestone, much more resistant to the wind-driven sand that blows in from the desert. The ancient master sculptor was able to use this stone to carve a masterpiece of Egyptian art that has survived the ravages of nature mostly intact. The damage to the face, resulting in the noseless icon so familiar to us today, was carried out purposefully by Arab iconoclasts sometime in the fifth century A.D.

There has been a great deal of debate and discussion about the Sphinx's beard. We know that the Sphinx once wore a beard, as pieces of it were discovered several centuries ago and are now housed in the Cairo Museum. In contrast to the trapezoidal royal beard worn by most other sphinxes, the beard of the Great Sphinx was long and curved, a divine beard of the type worn by gods. The only other place where this type of beard is seen on a sphinx is in reliefs from the 5th Dynasty. Some scholars have suggested that this beard dates not from the Old Kingdom, when the statue was carved, but from the New Kingdom, when repairs were made to the statue. The most recent geological studies strongly suggest that the beard is in fact from the Old Kingdom, and was part of the original limestone outcropping from which the Sphinx was carved.

Even without this confirmation, it is hard to imagine that the beard could have been added later as a separate piece, as it would have been extremely difficult to attach properly.

In 1983, due to concern among officials in the Egyptian Antiquities Organization (EAO) that the Sphinx's head was in danger, a suggestion was made that the beard should be restored in order to support the head. No scientific study was involved and the fear was based entirely on superficial information and not on technical or geological evidence. In 1989, UNESCO commissioned a scientific investigation by a French institution to examine the head and the area of the Sphinx's neck. The UNESCO team used ultrasonic techniques for this purpose. In addition, they took samples from different locations on the body for chemical analysis in order to get a more accurate diagnosis of the surface weathering.

One of the most important results of their work was to show that the neck and the head of the Great Sphinx are actually the strongest part of the statue. The conclusion was that the reconstruction of the beard was not needed to support the head. I was very glad about this, since I did not feel that reconstructing the beard from the pieces remaining would be effective, and because it would change the familiar image we know today much too drastically. However, one positive result of this discussion was that photogrammetric maps were made of the Sphinx; these have helped us to reconstruct the original appearance of this important monument.

Once the body of the Sphinx had been roughly cut into the bedrock, the Old Kingdom sculptors used fine-quality limestone blocks from Tura to finish the lion's form. These blocks were used to case the body; and the details of the body, paws, and tail were carved into them, rather than into the poor-quality mother rock. Many of these blocks fell away and were put back or replaced by various ancient and modern efforts at reconstruction over the millennia, most recently during our 1988–1998 Sphinx Conservation Project.

It is interesting to notice that the body of the Great Sphinx is much longer than it should be in proportion to its width and the size of the head. This tells us both that the exact location of the statue was of paramount importance and that the Egyptians understood the geology of the bedrock. Thus they were able to isolate the rock core in a way that would allow the sculptors to carve the head into the harder Member III stratum that ran above the weaker rock of Members I and II.

The Date of the Sphinx

There are a number of theories about the date of the Great Sphinx. Some pseudoscientists and charlatans would like you to believe that it was carved ten thousand years ago, when people from the mythical land of Atlantis (a culture for which there is absolutely no evidence) came to Egypt after their home was destroyed by natural disasters. They cite all sorts of scientific-sounding data about weathering and flooding, and bring in stellar alignment and other kinds of "proof." But their arguments are all specious (for example, they fail to understand the distinctions between the various strata of rock into which the statue is carved) and have been convincingly disproven. Other people invent imaginary aliens from outer space; these theories tend to be totally ridiculous and are really useful only for their entertainment value.

And there is, in fact, a great deal of evidence about when the Sphinx was carved: it all points to the 4th Dynasty, c. 2600 B.C. The head represents a king wearing the traditional Egyptian nemes headdress with the rearing cobra of royalty (the uraeus); onto his chin was strapped the curving false beard of divinity. Our recent excavations even uncovered ancient tools, identical to those used by the 4th Dynasty Egyptians, that were used to carve the head and neck of the Sphinx.

Most scholars believe, as I do, that the Sphinx represents Khafre and forms an integral part of his pyramid complex, a theory that dates back to Gaston Maspero, second head of the Egyptian Antiquities Service. Recently, a very important and comprehensive study of the Sphinx dates it to the time of Khafre. However, another school of Egyptologists, led by Rainer Stadelmann, believes that the Sphinx represents Khufu rather than Khafre.

Unfortunately, we do not have any contemporary texts to tell us who carved the Sphinx. We do have one important later text relating to it, the Inventory Stele, also known as the Stele of Khufu's Daughter. We spoke of this stele earlier, in our discussion of Khufu's subsidiary pyramid GI-c (see p. 91). To refresh your memory, this stele is located in the Late Period (between about 700 and 500 B.C.) Isis temple built on the remains of the eastern chapel of this small pyramid. The relevant portion of this text, which dates to the period of this temple (we know this from the style of the scenes and the grammar of the text), almost two thousand years after the death of Khufu, states that Khufu had established the Isis temple beside the house of the Sphinx, northwest of the house of Osiris, and then built his pyramid beside this temple.

As you can imagine, much is made of this stele by the believers in aliens and/or people from Atlantis. However, two thousand years is a long time, and we must give more credence to the clear and irrefutable archaeological and geological evidence than to this isolated text. It is very nice when textual and archaeological evidence match, but this is often not the case, especially when there is a large time lag between the one and the other. However, let me emphasize again that *all* Egyptologists date the Sphinx to the 4th Dynasty, and that the debate is between Khufu and Khafre, with no reference whatsoever to other possibilities.

There are many reasons to assign the Sphinx to Khafre rather than Khufu. To start with, the face of the Sphinx resembles the face seen on statues of Khafre. The Khufu camp claims the opposite, but there are no certain contemporary images of Khufu, so there is really no useful evidence to evaluate. The one surviving image of this king may date to the 26th Dynasty, and in any case the features of this statue do not match the features of the Sphinx.

The location of the Sphinx, at the entrance to Khafre's complex,

indicates clearly that it is meant to be understood as a colossal representation of this king. The archaeology of the site also supports this identification. The south side of the U-shaped Sphinx ditch forms the northern
edge of Khafre's causeway as it runs past the Sphinx and enters the Khafre
valley temple. A drainage channel runs along the north side of the causeway and opens into the upper southwest corner of the Sphinx ditch, indicating that the causeway was carved before the Sphinx ditch was
completed.

An early theory, accepted without question by many Egyptologists,
is that Khafre's overseer of all works turned a random outcropping of
rock into a statue to resemble Khafre with the face of a king and the
body of a lion. Recent analysis carried out by Mark Lehner, however,
has led him to the conclusion that the location of the Sphinx was chosen very carefully in relation to the pyramid of Khafre. I believe that
when the ancient Egyptians quarried limestone from the Sphinx area to
build the superstructures of Khafre's pyramid complex, the overseer of
works (perhaps Ankhhaf himself) had the idea for the Sphinx already in
mind and ordered that an outcropping of stone be left standing in this
particular place. Thus the master plan for Khafre's complex would have
included the Sphinx as an important component.

The Great Sphinx faces east, toward the rising sun; and nestled before its paws is a small temple known simply as the Sphinx temple. The
relationships between Khafre's pyramid temples and the Sphinx temple
also link the Sphinx to Khafre: Khafre's valley temple sits on the same
rock-cut terrace as the Sphinx temple. The fronts and backs of the temples are nearly aligned and the walls of both are built in the same style—
large limestone blocks with harder red granite added as a finish, and
there is evidence that these limestone blocks were quarried from the
Sphinx ditch itself. The Sphinx temple had an open central court filled
with ten colossal statues arranged around its periphery. Herbert Ricke, a
Swiss Egyptologist who carried out a detailed study of the Sphinx temple from 1967 to 1970, pointed out that this court was nearly an exact

copy of the one in Khafre's mortuary temple, except the latter had twelve colossal statues instead of ten.

The Meaning of the Great Sphinx

We have no contemporary texts that tell us directly about the meaning of the Sphinx. The name "sphinx" was given to this statue, and to the many smaller versions of the recumbent lion with a king's head that have survived to this day from ancient Egypt, by the Greeks. The Greek sphinx was a very different creature, with a woman's head, the wings of an eagle, the body of a lion, and the tale of a snake, but it was similar enough that the Hellenic mercenaries and travelers who first encountered the Egyptian version confused it with their own creation. The Greek name does, however, seem to be derived from the Egyptian name for this type of statue, *shespu*.

All the later texts associated with the Great Sphinx confirm that this statue was identified as a god. In the New Kingdom, it became an important focus for a popular and royal cult under the name Horemakhet ("Horus in the horizon"), a combination of the god of kingship, Horus, and the sun god Re. The image of the Sphinx between the pyramids of Khafre and Khufu provides a graphic illustration of this concept, as expressed by the hieroglyph for the *akhet*: the two pyramids resemble the two mountains of the horizon with the Sphinx as the setting sun disk in between.

The Sphinx was also known by the name Haroun, a Semitic name that may have been given to it by the Canaanites who came to Egypt in the reign of Amenhotep II. It was also called Du-hor, meaning "the palace of Horus," and the Arabic Abou Houl ("Father of Fear") was derived from this name.

We have other clues to the meaning of the Sphinx. For example, we know from the Pyramid Texts that during the Old Kingdom, the king was identified with the earth god Atum, the creator god associated with the sun god Re at Heliopolis. The Sphinx, which grows organically from the earth itself, is a perfect model of the chthonic Atum, who himself emerged from the earth at the beginning of time.

The Sphinx temple also offers clues to the meaning of the Sphinx for its Old Kingdom builders. Its central feature was an open court surrounded by a covered colonnade whose roof was supported by twenty-four square granite pillars. There were two sanctuaries, one on the east and another on the west, aligned on the center axis of the temple. Ricke believed it was perhaps an early sun temple and that the Sphinx was a depiction of the sun god. He understood the architecture of the temple as symbolic of the circuit of the sun: the eastern sanctuary for the rising sun, the western for the setting sun, with each colonnade pillar symbolizing one of the twenty-four hours of the day and night.

It is interesting to note that during the equinoxes the east-west axis of the Sphinx temple aligns, over the Sphinx's shoulder, with the sun's setting point at the south foot of Khafre's pyramid. This alignment is yet another element tying the Sphinx to the Khafre pyramid complex, and one of the several indications that the Sphinx is not an ad hoc creation for a block of unused stone in a quarry of Khufu.

My personal belief is that the concept of the Sphinx is related to the new solar cult of Khufu. The Great Sphinx, according to my theory, represents Khafre as Horus, facing east to worship his father, Khufu, as the sun god Re. The Sphinx temple is thus dedicated to Khufu, and Khafre is the eternal actor in the perpetual cult.

Chapter Fourteen

The Court of Khafre

It could be exhausting being Horus on earth. Before he had become king, he had

only one wife; now he had several, and had to balance their needs and desires, and

the competing claims of their children. He was getting on in years and didn't know

how much longer he could hold on. Several of his younger brothers were still hoping

for their own turns on the throne of their father. If he could choose, he would make

his young son Menkaure his heir, but Menkaure's mother, Khamerernebty, was very

young, and they would never be able to hold on to power. Perhaps he could enlist

the support of his brothers, promise them that they could sit on the Great Throne

in return for their promise to support the boy—neither of them would live for long

after his own death.

We know that Khafre's family life, like that of his father, must have been fairly complex. He probably had several brothers and half brothers still living, and we know that he had at least three wives and sixteen children. It is interesting that his complex contains no queens' pyramids.

Perhaps all of his spouses outlived him, or perhaps he did not want to favor one over another.

For example, his queen Mersyankh III is buried in a beautiful tomb, G7530+40, in the eastern cemetery, rather than in a small pyramid. It may be this was due somehow to a continuing struggle between the Djedefre and Khafre branches of the family, but we do not know for certain. In any case, Queen Mersyankh III was the daughter of Prince Kawab, eldest son of Khufu, and Hetepheres II. She outlived her husband (which may be why she was not buried in a pyramid) and died at the age of fifty. Her tomb is beautifully inscribed and decorated with scenes and statues cut into the living rock, and it provides us with a good deal of material on the royal family, religious beliefs, mummification, and other customs of the 4th Dynasty Egyptians.

Within her tomb, Mersyankh III is represented wearing a form-fitting dress that reaches to her ankles; in at least one scene, she holds a lotus flower, symbol of eternal rebirth, to her nose. Her mother, Hetepheres II, and her father, Kawab, are also depicted in the tomb, as are many other relatives. The scenes on the walls include artisans with blowpipes melting gold and making faience; sculptors carving a sarcophagus; men dragging statues; musicians, singers, and dancers; activities related to agriculture; a pilgrimage to the sacred site of Abydos; and Mersyankh and her mother boating on the marshes. Most of these scenes fall into the category usually referred to as "scenes of daily life"; as I have mentioned, all the scenes in the tomb carry religious significance at some level and function to ensure both the eternal life of the deceased and the proper functioning of the Egyptian cosmos. At the same time, they provide us with enormous amounts of information about the rich and vibrant lives led by the ancient Egyptians.

An inscription at the entrance to the tomb tells us that 272 days passed between the death of Mersyankh III and her burial. This is unusual: mummification normally took seventy-two days, so there was evidently some delay whose cause must remain a mystery.

Unique to this tomb and only a few others from this period is a series of ten rock-cut statues: four of Mersyankh herself, three of her mother, and three of her daughters. Her sarcophagus bears an inscription telling us that it was presented to her by her mother. With Khafre, she bore a son named Duwanera, who was later to serve as vizier to Menkaure, Khafre's son by another queen. Duwanera bore the title "eldest son of Khafre," but he did not succeed his father. This lends credence to the theory that it was not necessarily the eldest son who inherited the throne.

Khafre's principal adviser seems to have been Ankhhaf, who may also have acted as an adviser to his father. This man, who was buried in the eastern cemetery in tomb G7510, the second largest in the field (after that of Kawab), bore the titles of vizier and overseer of all the king's work. I believe that he lived to be an old man during Khafre's reign, as his grandson Ankhetef is shown in his tomb. He was married to a king's (perhaps Khufu's) eldest daughter.

We can imagine that Ankhhaf was the most important man in the country after the king. He may have directed political affairs in the country and was most likely responsible for the design of the pyramid complex. Although he could not have directly supervised the daily work on the complex, he would have chosen the layout and set up the procedures for the overseers to follow.

Another vizier of Khafre's was Minkhaf, also a king's son. Scholars believe that he was the son of Khufu by Henutsen, the queen buried in the southernmost pyramid east of the Great Pyramid. Perhaps Minkhaf was the architect who made Ankhhaf's ideas come alive and supervised the construction of the pyramid. The other important official who would have assisted with the building of the pyramid was Neferma'at II, third vizier of Khafre, who was buried on the east side of the pyramid in tomb G7060. Neferma'at's mother was named Nefertkau; she is thought to have been a daughter of Sneferu and a minor queen. Her daughter, Nefertkau II, was married to Khafkhufu I (who may have become Khafre).

Late in his reign, Khafre seems to have married another queen, named Khedhekhnu, with whom he had a son named Sekhemkare. This child lived into the 5th Dynasty, and served as vizier under Userkaf (c. 2513–2506 B.C.) before dying during the reign of Sahure. The reason that scholars believe he was the son of Khafre is because of the location of his tomb east of the pyramid of Khafre.

There are many other interesting tombs at Giza that date to the reign of Khafre. For example, there was a woman named Meretyetes III who was a priestess of the cults of Khufu, Hathor, and Neith. She was a daughter of Khufu and the wife of a man named Akhet-hotep, who also bore the title of priest of Khufu. The fact that this title was held by a royal daughter is an indication of the importance of the role of the priest or priestess of the royal cult during the 4th Dynasty. Nisedjerkai, another woman buried at Giza, was also a priestess of Khufu and Hathor.

Several of the tombs we discovered recently in the western cemetery of Khufu most likely date to the reign of Khafre, although they do not belong to members of the royal family. One of these is the tomb of the dwarf Perniankhu, who bore the title "dwarf of the palace, who pleases his majesty every day." Dwarfs in Egypt are known to have performed special dances, and it is likely that Perniankhu performed sacred dances for the amusement of the king. Within a sealed statue chamber attached to his tomb, we found a beautiful statue. I believe that this man was the father of another dwarf buried nearby in a larger tomb; the son's name is Seneb, and he was a high government official who served as a priest of several 4th Dynasty kings as well as acting as a tutor of the king's children.

Another 4th Dynasty tomb, beautifully carved and painted with vibrantly colored scenes, belonged to a priest of the royal cult and senior scribe named Kay. A fascinating glimpse into an ancient economic exchange is offered by an inscription at the entrance to this tomb, which reads: "It is the tomb makers, the draftsmen, the craftsmen, and the sculptors who made my tomb. I paid them in bread and beer and made them take an oath that they were satisfied."

Apart from the information offered by his pyramid complex and the tombs of his courtiers, we know little else of Khafre's reign. We do know that he sent a number of expeditions to Nubia to bring diorite and granite for the construction of his temple and statues. Also, the names of Khufu, Khafre, and Menkaure have been found at Byblos, indicating that all three kings were trading with the Syro–Palestinian coastal cities. The name of Khafre was also found at the site of Ebla in Syria, which indicates some sort of relationship with the countries east of the Mediterranean.

Chapter Fifteen

The Death of Khafre

The old king Khufu had thrown a long shadow in life, and he was not finished.
Two more of his chief princes were still alive and awaiting their turns on the throne.
There was no greater claim to the rule of the Two Lands than the blood of King
Khufu, and Khafre's young heir, Menkaure, was not yet old enough to ascend the
throne. So it was his brother Djedefre who laid Khafre to rest within his gleaming
pyramid and performed the rites that would send his ka to join the other gods.

*M*ost histories of the Old Kingdom list Menkaure directly after
Khafre. However, there is some evidence for a series of ephemeral kings
between the builders of the second and third pyramids at Giza. Manetho
lists a king named Bicheris as the successor of Khafre and reports that
he ruled for only four years. The Middle Kingdom graffito in the
Wadi Hammamat that I have mentioned before, written by officials
from Memphis, records the following sequence of 4th Dynasty kings
(the names all written inside cartouches): Khufu, Djedefre, Khafre,
Djedefhor(re), Baufre. This is usually assumed to be incorrect, a mistake
made by pious priests of a credulous period, and more credence is put

in the later, more official king lists. However, although the text is meant as a list of offering recipients, rather than a historical king list, it is the text closest in time to the actual events of the Old Kingdom, and may be accurate.

The Bicheris of Manetho's list can tentatively be identified with Baufre of the Wadi Hammamat list. This man also appears in the Westcar Papyrus as one of the sons of Khufu. I believe that he may be the same as Baufhor, who is thought to have been a son of Khufu and was buried in one of the large mastabas at Giza. Baufhor held the rank of vizier and was married to the princess Mersyankh II, a daughter of Khufu, who was also buried in the same mastaba. We know from her titles that she was the wife of a king, and it is often assumed that this was Khafre. However, if the theory that Baufhor became Baufre and ruled for a short time as king, then Mersyankh's title would have come from the man we know was her husband. If Baufre ever did reign, his time on the throne was so short that almost nothing is known about him.

Djedefhor as we have mentioned is almost certainly the same as the Dedefhor/Hordedef who appears in the Westcar Papyrus as Khufu's son, the prince who escorts the magician Djedi to the palace. This man was remembered by later Egyptians as the author of a set of instructions, advice on how to live properly. He was buried at Giza in tomb G7320, east of the Great Pyramid.

We do not have any certain monuments of Hordedef and Baufre that prove that they were kings. One of them may have started a pyramid complex at Zawiet el-Aryan, where there is an unattributed pyramid of about the right period. But if either or both of them did reign, they left little on the ground in terms of royal monuments and thus have been relegated to the back pages of history. It is the next king, Menkaure, who left his mark, building the smallest, but in many ways the most beautiful, of the pyramids at Giza.

Chapter Sixteen

Menkaure Ascends the Throne

The death of Hordedef was not unexpected, as he was old and had been ailing for some time. But his rule, short as it was, was wise, and he made sure that all Egypt was ready to accept the new king that he had chosen. Of the many grandsons of Khufu, Prince Menkaure stood out from the rest. A son of Khafre, he was young and vigorous but already wise beyond his years. It was as if the gods had touched him with greatness; in him lay the genius of diplomacy, just what was needed to reconcile the warring factions within the royal family. He had studied with the priests at Heliopolis and was certain to make peace with them too.

At some point after the death of his father, Khafre, Menkaure ascended the throne of Egypt. In addition to his cartouche name, he took the Two Ladies name, Khakhet ("His body is a bull"), and the Horus of Gold name Hor-nub-netjer ("Divine Horus of gold"). His name in Greek became Minkheris (from Manetho) or Mycerinus (as reported by Herodotus).

We know that Menkaure was the son of Khafre and a queen; we

think that she was probably Khamerernebty I. His sister, Khamerernebty II, is thought to have served as his principal queen; if Khamerernebty I was his mother, then Khamerernebty II would have been his full sister, and this would have been a good way to keep power concentrated in one branch of the family.

Manetho tells us that Menkaure ruled for sixty-three years; the Turin Canon, which reports an eighteen-year reign, is more likely to be accurate. Herodotus's guides remembered Menkaure kindly, reporting that he had reopened the temples closed by his grandfather and father and allowed the common people to return to giving offerings to the gods. He was remembered for his just rule; legend had it that if there was an official who was unhappy with a judgment of the court, Menkaure would compensate him from his own treasury to keep him happy. However, the gods of Egypt ruled that the land should suffer and the good king was given only six years to live. Menkaure doubled his allotted time on earth by staying awake all night. This tale was the subject of a poem titled "Myccrinus," written in 1849 by Matthew Arnold.

The Pyramid of Menkaure

Menkaure chose the southern edge of the Giza plateau as the site for his pyramid, which he named "Menkaure is divine." For some reason, he planned a much smaller monument than that of his father or grandfather (one tenth the size of the Great Pyramid). Many scholars believe that this was for economic reasons, but the sixteen lower courses of the pyramid were cased with granite, an extremely expensive stone. It is possible that the original plan was to case the entire structure in granite; however, Menkaure's complex was far from finished when he died. It was completed by his son and successor, Shepseskaf, who cased the rest of the pyramid in limestone (and finished the temples in mud brick).

We do not know why Menkaure chose granite for the casing of his pyramid. It is much more difficult to work with than limestone and would have slowed down the work enormously. However, it is clear that a great architect was in charge of the project, as the layout and execution of the pyramid and its complex were very well done.

At the entrance to the pyramid, carved on a patch of the granite casing, is an inscription stating that Menkaure died on the twenty-third day of the fourth month of summer. The regnal year, unfortunately, is not given, but the text does tell us that the king was buried with rich funerary equipment. This inscription does not date from the Old Kingdom but was added in the New Kingdom or Late Period. Most likely it was carved during the reign of Rameses II, whose son Khaemwaset was fascinated by the ancient kings who had ruled before. This man served as high priest at Memphis and restored many of the Old Kingdom monuments in the area.

The entrance, in the north face of the pyramid, leads through a descending passage, lined for much of its length with granite, to a rectangular antechamber under the earth, with niches carved into the bedrock that forms its walls. A horizontal passage, blocked by granite portcullises, leads to a rectangular burial chamber beneath the center of the pyramid. A second system of passages leads to a blocked entrance, perhaps evidence that the superstructure was originally planned to be even smaller.

At some point, two more chambers, approached by a ramp in the floor of the first burial chamber and then by a crude set of steps, were added beneath the original substructure. The first of these chambers has six deep niches roughly carved into its walls, four on the east and two on the north. Scholars have suggested that these were for the interment of the canopic jars or the royal crowns, or perhaps for equipment used in the burial ritual. I believe that these were equivalent to underground food and drink storage cellars, such as might have existed in the houses of the living, and that they were stocked with food and drink offerings for the afterlife. The second chamber on this level was lined with granite, and probably served as the actual burial chamber.

In the original burial chamber, the pyramid's first modern explorer,

Richard Howard Vyse, found the lid of a wooden sarcophagus bearing an inscription for "Osiris Menkaure." This has been dated stylistically to the Late Period. Nearby were linen wrappings and some human bones, which themselves have been radiocarbon dated to early Christian times. Perhaps some sort of symbolic reburial was carried out when the later inscription was carved near the entrance.

Against the western wall of the second, granite-lined burial chamber, Vyse found an empty basalt sarcophagus decorated on the outside with niched paneling. With difficulty, he had the sarcophagus removed from the pyramid and transported to Alexandria, where it was loaded aboard a ship named the *Beatrice*, bound for England. Unfortunately, the *Beatrice* sank to the bottom of the Mediterranean near the coast of Spain in 1838, taking the sarcophagus with it. It would be wonderful if some of the underwater archaeologists who work in the western Mediterranean would go and look for this sunken treasure!

Menkaure's complex, as completed by Shepseskaf, gives us a great deal of information about royal funerary cults in general and his cult in particular. His priesthood was active through the Old Kingdom, for at least three hundred years. The complex was excavated in the early to mid-1900s by one of the great pioneers of archaeology, George Reisner; discovered within Menkaure's temples were a large number of statues, which rank among the greatest sculptures of the Old Kingdom.

The complex is entered, like the others, through a valley temple, one that lies significantly farther west than the temples of Khufu or Khafre. The original plan of the temple was organized around a central court, with an entrance hall flanked by small rooms to the east and storage magazines and cult rooms to the west.

Remains of a village housing the priests who served Menkaure's cult have been excavated in the area around and inside his lower temple. Part of this village was excavated by Reisner, who uncovered eleven small mud-brick houses and round granaries; there are more buildings here that remain to be uncovered. Artifacts found in the houses of the priests include pottery types spanning the 4th to 6th Dynasties. Reisner believed that the earliest houses were built inside the courtyard of the lower temple and that the city continued to expand from this area. It is more likely, however, that the houses for Menkaure's priests were originally built outside the lower temple and only later, probably in the 5th Dynasty, spread up over the eastern wall and into the courtyard inside the temple.

It is clear from the archaeological evidence that a rough-and-ready cult was being carried out in the valley temple in the later Old Kingdom, focused on a dingy chamber at the back of the tightly packed village of mud brick. At some point, possibly near the end of the 5th Dynasty, torrents of water washed down through a neighboring wadi and destroyed the western part of the temple. A new temple was built above the ruins of the old, probably at the beginning of the 6th Dynasty. A decree from the reign of Pepi II was discovered in the vestibule of the temple; it exempts the priests living here from paying taxes as long as they served the cult of the king. Menkaure's cult was maintained in this temple until the end of the Old Kingdom.

Inside a corridor at the back of the valley temple, Reisner discovered a great masterpiece of Egyptian art. This unfinished "pair statue," or dyad, carved from basalt, depicts Menkaure with a queen, presumably his principal wife. Unfortunately, the sculptor never inscribed their names and titles on its base. It shows the royal pair, standing to three-quarters life size, at equal scale, demonstrating their equal importance. The two statues are carved against a high back slab. The pair is integrated by the action of the queen, who places one arm around her husband's waist and the other on his arm. Both the king and the queen stride forward, left leg first.

This pair statue gives us insight into the court and religion of Menkaure, a court where the queen was equal in importance to the king. The fact that the queen is striding forward, in a typically male pose, underlines this equality. The loving relationship between the married couple shines forth from the hard stone and gives us a glimpse into the humanity of this king.

A number of other important statue groups were found in the valley temple. Key among these is a series of five graywacke triads (one of which is fragmentary), each of which shows Menkaure with two deities. Four of these depict Menkaure in the white crown of Upper Egypt, standing and striding forward, flanked on one side by Hathor (also striding forward and at the same scale) and on the other by the tutelary god or goddess of a specific Egyptian nome (province). Each of these groups is carved in extremely high relief, almost in the round, against a very high back slab.

The fifth triad is extremely unusual in that the central position is occupied by Hathor, seated on a throne. The king stands to her left, wearing a kilt and the crown of Upper Egypt, holding a ceremonial mace in his right hand and a small enigmatic object in his left hand; a nome goddess stands to Hathor's right. Hathor embraces the king with one arm around his waist and the other on his arm, just as the queen embraces him in the pair statue. What is unique about this statue group is that Hathor is shown at a larger scale than the king himself: seated, her head reaches the same height as that of the standing king.

Hathor is both a celestial and earthly divinity. She is the divine mother goddess. Her name is written with the falcon of Horus, god of kingship, within a rectangle, the hieroglyph for mansion or estate. Thus she is literally the estate of Horus, perhaps a reference to the kingship passing through the female line of the royal family and to her role as the queen mother, the "house" of the king during his period of gestation within her womb.

These five statue groups are clearly related to the provisioning of the king's cult, serving the same purpose as the images of the nome deities bearing offerings found on the walls of Sneferu's valley temple. The inscriptions before the figures of Hathor and the nome deities confirm this, as they read: "I have given to you every good thing and all offerings from the south as you are manifest as king of Upper and Lower Egypt forever." All of the nomes represented are from Upper Egypt, and the king wears the white crown of this region. There were probably more triads (perhaps as many as eight or sixteen), and some of these would most likely have represented Lower Egyptian nomes, with the king in the red crown. It has been suggested that there was one triad for each of Hathor's major cult centers.

The presence of Hathor also carries conceptions of fecundity and assurances of eternal rebirth. Hathor was extremely important to the royal cult. The principal queen was seen as an incarnation of this goddess, just as the king embodied Horus in life and Re in death. Hathor wears a sun disk, symbol of her father, Re, on her head, thus emphasizing the importance of the solar principle. These triads reinforce my contention that the lower temple was dedicated to the king as Horus and to the queen as Hathor, the eyes of Re and mother of the living king and the king to come.

Apart from their religious significance, all these statues are absolute masterpieces, beautifully carved and polished, and were once painted in vibrant colors. The Egyptians believed that painting the statues brought them to life, literally, as figures that could perform favors such as bringing in offerings and sustenance in the afterlife.

The king, queen, and divinities are all portrayed in an extremely idealized fashion, as is typical of the royal art of the Old Kingdom. The king has the body of an athletic adolescent, like the body of an Olympic champion swimmer. The sculptor has paid a good deal of attention to details such as the musculature in his legs. The sheer, skintight dresses worn by the queen and the goddesses reveal as much as they conceal; even the nipples are carved into the stone.

The faces of these statues are not usually considered portraiture in the sense in which we understand it today. Each figure has basically the same features, and it is generally assumed that the face shown is a generalized version of the king's face, used for any royal or divine figure. The king's fleshy proud nose, full cheeks, prominent eyeballs, and faint smile are all typical of Menkaure's other statues, idealized versions of his actual features. However, the similarity of the queen's features may be due, at least in part, to the fact that she was her husband's sister. The faces of Hathor and the nome goddesses resemble that of the queen because she embodied these divinities; the single male nome god depicted in the triads has quite a different face.

Menkaure's causeway ran straight from his valley temple to the mortuary temple that sits against the east face of his pyramid. This causeway was never completed, although its intended path can still be traced.

Menkaure's architects and engineers began building his mortuary temple with gigantic core blocks of locally quarried limestone, the largest of which weighs over two hundred tons. The temple is divided into two parts. The front part, the more public area, consists of an entrance hall and an open court. The private, or inner, part of the temple extends between the enclosure wall and the eastern face of the pyramid. The inner temple contained magazines arranged to the north and south of a long hall. In the southern magazines were the objects used in Menkaure's cult, such as offering vessels, model dishes, and stone vessels. In the northern magazines were the sorts of objects that the king would have once used in his palace and that he would need for his afterlife— pottery, flint knives, and wooden fragments that suggest the one-time presence of tables, games, boxes, chairs, and the like. The long hall served as the sanctuary, the focus of the cult; I believe that it held a statue or cult object of Re or a statue of Menkaure.

Reisner found an alabaster colossus of the king, now in the Boston Museum of Fine Arts, that he believed might once have stood at the back of this hall. The statue was originally almost 2.35 meters (7.7 feet) high. The king wears the royal nemes headdress, a kilt of pleated linen, and the false beard as a symbol of royalty. He holds a folded cloth in his right hand. The statue has a painted chin strap for the false beard, and a thin mustache was painted above his upper lip. The head is noticeably small in proportion to the rest of the body. An American Egyptologist named Peter Lacovera has suggested that the royal sculptors recarved the head to change the original design of the headdress or because of a flaw in the stone.

If it stood at the back of the central hall, the alabaster colossus of Menkaure would have faced down the axis of the temple causeway. Behind the statue, between the upper temple and the face of the pyramid, an inner offering chapel probably contained an emplacement for a false door, symbolic of the king's exit and entrance to the netherworld of the pyramid. The colossus would thus have represented the king emerging from the netherworld, facing down the causeway toward his pyramid town and the continuing passage of life in the Nile valley.

No boat pits have as yet been found associated with the pyramid of Menkaure. In the 1970s, the Egyptian archaeologist Abdel Aziz Saleh cleared an area near the north wall of the mortuary temple, expecting to find boats. He found that the mud-brick pavement overlay a bed of gravel above a layer of megalithic limestone blocks joined with mortar. Among the quarry marks on these blocks were four elaborate drawings of boats. Although partial removal of these blocks revealed nothing, Saleh believed that Menkaure's boats lay below this pavement, although the blocks do not resemble the long slabs of fine limestone that cover Khufu's southern boat pits. The boats drawn by the quarrymen, rather than depicting royal boats for Menkaure's cult, may be drawings of the boats used by the workmen when they transported stones for the pyramid.

I recently carried out some clearance work to the south of Menkaure's pyramid, looking for boat pits and also recording the location of fallen granite casing blocks as part of a project to restore them to their original places. One of my assistants, Allah Shahat, uncovered some limestone blocks that appear similar to the blocks covering Khufu's southern boat pits, and he thought that we might have found Menkaure's boat pits. But further excavation confirmed my suspicion that these blocks were simply the pavement of the pyramid court, the sacred area surrounding the pyramid that was entered only by certain priests in charge of the cult of the king.

Perhaps further clearance in the areas to the west and south of the main pyramid, which are still filled with stone rubble and fallen granite casing stones, will uncover Menkaure's boat pits. However, it is also possible that the king died before his boat pits were cut and that his son Shepseskaf never ordered them constructed.

Menkaure's complex contains three subsidiary pyramids, lined up east to west just south of the inner enclosure wall of his main pyramid, like sentinels guarding his southern flank. On the eastern side of each small pyramid is a small mud-brick temple. Reisner was able to trace the path of a wall enclosing the three pyramids, running a few meters outside the pyramid bases.

The easternmost pyramid, GIII-a, was finished as a true pyramid, with smooth sides. Most Egyptologists believe that this pyramid was Menkaure's ritual, or cult, pyramid, the equivalent of Khafre's southern pyramid or the small pyramid I recently discovered in Khufu's complex. This pyramid was first entered in 1881 by Richard Howard Vyse, who left a graffito inside recording his discovery. The substructure of this pyramid is T-shaped, like that of Khufu's ritual pyramid, and the burial chamber was left unfinished, also supporting its identification as a cult pyramid.

However, a number of other details suggest that at some point the royal house used the pyramid for an actual burial, perhaps of one of Menkaure's queens. The primary evidence for this theory is that an elaborate memorial chapel was built against its eastern face. A granite sarcophagus was fit into the burial chamber, and a portcullis was used to close the connecting corridor between the descending passage and the burial chamber. In the offering hall of the chapel, Reisner found fragments of a beautiful alabaster statue of a queen. It bore no inscription, so her identity remains a mystery. Model cups also found here bear the name of a king's son, Kay, perhaps left here as votives. Khamerernebty II seems a likely choice for the pyramid's occupant, but without an inscription, this cannot be proven. A large rock-cut tomb behind Khafre's valley temple has also been tentatively identified as the burial place of this queen.

During recent clearance around the base of this pyramid, my team at Giza found a double statue that New Kingdom sculptors were fashioning from a fallen granite block, 3.5 tons in weight, that had once been used to case this pyramid. Two images, whom I believe to be Rameses II, are roughed out in the ancient stone: one depicts him as a king, and the other shows him as a god. We know from inscriptions left at the site that members of Rameses' court and administration were active at Giza, and it is likely that his sculptors chose to use this readily available block of stone rather than sending all the way to Aswan for a fresh slab. However, while the statue was still in its preliminary stages, the block cracked, and it was abandoned where it lay, with sculptors' tools still left scattered about for us to discover.

The central and western small pyramids (GIII-b and GIII-c) were built as step pyramids. The substructures display the typical characteristics of queens' pyramids, with a turn from the entrance passage into the burial chamber. If GIII-a was originally designed as Menkaure's cult pyramid, GIII-b must have been for the leading lady at court and GIII-c for the second most important queen.

Against the west wall of the stone-lined burial chamber of GIII-b, Vyse found a plain red granite sarcophagus containing some bones, including the jawbone and teeth of a young woman, along with rotted wood and fragments of bandages. The burial chamber of GIII-c, like that of GIII-a, was left unfinished and contained no sarcophagus, but Reisner found hundreds of votive vessels inside its eastern chapel. Thus a queen must have been buried here. In fact, the temple of GIII-c is more elaborate than the temple of GIII-b, where a burial is well in evidence within the burial chamber.

Excavations begun in 1980 by the late Egyptian Egyptologist Abdel Aziz Saleh uncovered an important site associated with Menkaure's complex, the so-called industrial community. This lies seventy meters (230 feet) south of the causeway of Menkaure in the main wadi that runs between the Mokattam and Maadi formations. Built against two embankments of stone rubble mixed with mortar, thought by Saleh to be connected with the transport ramps necessary for the building of the complex, were fifteen buildings of various sizes. These include large ovens—some for baking bread, others for firing ceramics; a hearth for metallurgy; an area for working faience; and some large pieces of alabaster and granite, perhaps the remains of a royal statuary workshop. The entire area was most likely devoted to workshops connected with Menkaure's pyramid complex and cult, where small objects for the daily cult rituals were fashioned and where fresh offerings were prepared. It is likely that mummification also took place in this area.

The Court of Menkaure

By the reign of Menkaure, the family of Khufu had proliferated into numerous branches. We do not know what gave Menkaure, above his many brothers and half brothers, the right to the throne of Egypt. Perhaps he was the strongest, or was the eldest (or youngest) son of Khafre's most important queen. As before, the rules of succession elude us, perhaps to be clarified someday by further research into the remarkable royal family of the 4th Dynasty. We know that Menkaure built his palace at Giza like his father and grandfather, although we do not know whether he built in the same location or not. But the pyramid cities of Giza must have been hard put to accommodate the needs of this sprawling family.

As is the case for much of Egyptian history, most of our information on the members of this family and of the court in general comes from their tombs. During the reign of Menkaure, members of Khafre's family began to utilize the Khufu-Khafre quarry to the southeast of the second pyramid for rock-cut tombs. These chapels, carved into the solid rock, allowed for a notable increase in tomb size that resulted in the expansion of traditional scenes of the 4th Dynasty mastaba chapels at Giza, especially of so-called scenes from daily life. There are also more statues and inscriptions from this period, and there seems to have been more freedom for people to carry out religious rites than before.

We know of a number of viziers who served Menkaure, all members of the royal family. Duwanera, son of Khafre and Mersyankh III and thus the half brother of Menkaure, would have been his first vizier, and most likely was responsible for planning his pyramid complex. Three other viziers, Min-yuwn, Akhmara, and Nekaure, seem to have been sons of Menkaure. Khunera, the son of Menkaure and Queen Khamer-ernebty II, does not tell us much about his role in the administration of the country in his tomb in the quarry of his father.

There is also evidence in the tombs which dates to this period that Menkaure began a new policy designed to increase the loyalty of the nobility to the royal house. He opened his palace to the children of high officials and allowed them to be trained with the royal sons; then when they grew up they would always be faithful to him and his heirs. One of these young nobles was a young man named Shepsesptah, whose tomb inscription brags that he was trained in the palace of the king.

Debhen, who was buried in a rock-cut tomb north of Menkaure's causeway, was a fairly high official in Menkaure's administration. His principal titles were secretary of the toilet house, overlord of Nekheb, and master of largesse in the mansion of life. An inscription in this tomb provides a glimpse into the trickle-down economy of 4th Dynasty Egypt: Debhen reports that he met Menkaure one day as the king was inspecting his pyramid. Seizing this opportunity, Debhen asked if the king would allow him to be buried near his pyramid. Menkaure agreed, and ordered that a tomb ten cubits (5.24 meters; 17 feet) long and fifty cubits (26.2 meters; 86 feet) wide be built for him, allotting fifty men for its construction, and even ordering his own architect to bring limestone from the royal quarry to build a large statue, two false doors, and blocks for the tomb facade. All these elements were discovered in Debhen's tomb, although the statue was in pieces. An interesting note: the text relates that this encounter occurred while Menkaure was beside the pyramid of "Her" on the way to his own pyramid. This must have been one of the other pyramids at Giza, but we do not know which one.

Debhen's tomb was later used by a Sufi (a practitioner of a mystical Islamic cult) named Sedi Hamad el-Samman. When this man died, the local people called the village near the pyramid Nazlet el-Samman, meaning the "place where el-Samman lived." The people of the village used this tomb for their Friday prayer meeting because of its connection with this holy man.

Another important official, named Ptahshepses, was born during the reign of Menkaure. This man may have been the half brother of Userkaf, the first king of the 5th Dynasty. He was buried at Abusir, the preferred site of the kings of this dynasty, and the titles in his tomb show that he reached the rank of vizier.

Most of the older generation of Menkaure's family died during the eighteenth year of Menkaure's reign, the year when we believe the king himself died. Perhaps a plague struck the capital.

Menkaure was succeeded by a king named Shepseskaf, who is assumed to have been his son. He was certainly pious and expended significant resources in completing his predecessor's complex, albeit in mud brick rather than limestone. A link between the two reigns is provided by Shepseskaf's vizier Babaef, buried in G5230, who was the son of Menkaure's vizier Duwanera.

Recent discoveries at Giza have opened a window onto the lives of an entirely different segment of society than the royal and elite men and women whose tombs have been the main focus of scholarly study for the past century or so. In 1990, the cemetery of the men and women who actually labored to build the pyramids came to light. This incredible find was followed by an equally startling discovery: the royal installation and town where these men and women lived and where their food and equipment was produced and distributed. Excavations in the pyramid builders' area, southeast of the main plateau at Giza, are ongoing, and wonderful discoveries are being made each year.

The installation now being uncovered (in excavations led by Mark Lehner) dates from the reigns of Khafre and Menkaure. It is likely that an earlier installation belonging to the workforce of Khufu was located here, but its remains were razed and dumped nearby, presumably when Khafre brought the court back to Giza. However, the information gleaned from this site is almost certainly valid for Khufu's reign as well. The cemetery was begun sometime in the 4th Dynasty, presumably in the reign of Khufu, and continued to be used on into the 5th and perhaps even the 6th Dynasty, serving the population of artisans and workmen responsible for building the later elite tombs on the plateau and servicing the royal cults that remained at Giza.

Part Four

The Pyramid
Builders at Giza

Chapter Seventeen

The Pyramid Builders of Giza

Neferhetepes lay down next to her husband on their mud-brick sleeping platform, exhausted from the hard work of the day. With any delivery, there was a danger of losing mother or child, and this had been a particularly difficult birth. The labor had lasted since the previous morning, all through the hours of the day and then through the dark and dangerous hours of the night, when strong magic had been needed to keep the demons from snatching the mother's breath from her body. But the baby had been born this day, when the sun god Re was high in the sky, smiling down at the exhausted woman as the new baby finally made his appearance. Neferhetepes' husband, Nefertheith, had been hard at work all day too, supervising many aspects of the care and feeding of the workers, from the baking of countless loaves of bread and brewing of vast oceans of beer to the feeding of the thousands of workers who toiled in the service of their divine king, to making sure that enough cattle were delivered from the royal estates. Despite their exhaustion, Neferhetepes and Nefertheith were grateful to have a moment together and turned to each other to review their days.

One of the most enduring myths about the Great Pyramid is that it was built by slaves. This is not true. Slavery, while it existed in ancient Egypt, was not an important part of the economy, especially in the Old Kingdom. The pyramids were the national project of Egypt, symbolizing the might and power of the ruling house, ensuring the rebirth of the king as a god, and thus magically maintaining the universe as it should be; the entire country would have participated in their erection, each extended family paying their dues by sending food, materials, and manpower. From hieroglyphic inscriptions and graffiti we infer that skilled builders and craftsmen probably worked year-round at the pyramid construction site. Peasant farmers from the surrounding villages and provinces rotated in and out of the labor force. The pyramid project must have been a tremendous socializing force in the early Egyptian kingdom—young conscripts from hamlets and villages far and wide taking leave of their families and traveling to Giza, then returning full of the latest ideas and fashions from the royal capital. The workforce would have swelled to its largest size during *akhet*, the season of the flood, when the fields lay under water and the farmers could not tend their crops. Careful census records would have been kept of every household in the land, and their contributions to the project would have been carefully noted.

A similar system is still in place in Egyptian villages today. When a member of the community builds a new house, the other families have to pay money to help him. The owner of the new house records every donation in a book, and when it is someone else's turn to build a house, he must offer the same or more money back. At lunch, every family in the village has to send a tray of food to feed the workmen building the house, and some households even send workers to participate in the project. When a villager is married, a collection organized along similar lines, called *nukta* ("payment" or "loan"), is taken and given to the groom.

Scholars have long known that an enormous support system must

have existed at Giza for at least sixty-seven years, the combined mini-
mum lengths of Khufu's, Khafre's, and Menkaure's reigns. Such support
would have included production facilities for food, ceramics, and building materials (gypsum, mortar, stone, wood, and metal); storage facilities
for food, fuel, and other supplies; and housing for the workmen and their
overseers. But until recently, there was no archaeological evidence for
this workforce; three generations of pyramid builders seemed to have
disappeared without a trace.

Herodotus was told by the guides who showed him the monuments
at Giza that one hundred thousand slaves toiled for twenty years to build
the Great Pyramid. A more reasonable estimate, based on scientific cal-
culations of the amount of stone that would have had to be moved per
day in order to finish the pyramid during Khufu's reign, is in the realm
of twenty thousand workers. By using the graffiti left behind by workmen in the quarries and on stones within the pyramids themselves, and
from analysis of elite titles, scholars have been able to reconstruct the basic organization of the pyramid workforce. Additional information has
come from two groups of royal archives dating to the 5th Dynasty, found
at the site of Abusir, and from new excavations at Giza.

The ultimate responsibility for the pyramid construction lay with
the vizier, who bore the title "overseer of all the king's work." Under
him were several overseers of the king's work, overseers of the work, and
then supervisors who held more specific titles, such as overseer of a
group of ten. The workmen themselves were divided into crews of two
thousand. Each crew was divided into two gangs of one thousand, each
with a name such as Friends of Khufu, or Menkaure Is Drunk. The
gangs were divided into five groups that we call phyles, from the Greek
word meaning tribe. These groups bore names such as Great/Starboard
Ones, Asiatic/Port Ones, or Green/Prow Ones. Each phyle consisted of
two hundred workmen supervised by an overseer. Within these groups,
smaller subdivisions of twenty to fifty men were given names such as

Life, Endurance, and Perfection. Competition among the various divisions would have been very important in boosting morale and accelerating the work.

All this had been put together from textual evidence, but there was no footprint on the ground, no archaeological data to support this reconstruction. But now we have found the pyramid builders of Giza. Since 1991, we have been excavating one of the most exciting and important archaeological discoveries ever made: the remains of the town where the permanent staff of artisans and supervisors lived, the royal installation where the temporary workmen were housed and fed, and the vast cemetery in which the pyramid builders were buried. These new discoveries have added exponentially to our understanding of how the pyramids were built.

As described earlier, the pyramid town came to light first in the 1980s, during soundings taken for the new sewage system installed under the suburb that lies at the foot of the plateau. We caught only glimpses of this town but found enough to ascertain that it stretches for several kilometers along the foot of the plateau. Khufu's palace, as mentioned before, lay close to his valley temple, at the north end of the plateau; the houses of his family and court, along with his administrative buildings, would most likely have been near his palace. The sewage trenches revealed only fragments of mud-brick walls and quantities of broken pottery, but even with this slender evidence, certain areas could sometimes be identified. One very large building of massive mud-brick walls and cleanly swept courts or rooms came to light. Fragments of limestone that may have come from wall-lining slabs, red granite chips, and much fine pottery suggest an elite building. It is tempting to imagine an important administrative center here, but unfortunately the evidence is not sufficient to prove it.

Another area yielded a concentration of beer jar fragments, indicating the remains of a brewery. Next to this, thousands of broken pottery bread molds, burnt clay, and ash-laden soil identified the area of a bakery. Similar remains came from a second bakery about a kilometer away. The area between these two bakeries yielded evidence of mud-brick housing, some quite ephemeral, others deeply stratified and suggesting longer periods of occupation. From the limited remains uncovered it is not possible to distinguish different sorts of housing.

I felt certain that there were more remains to be discovered of the pyramid builders at Giza, and in 1988, I came back from my graduate studies in the United States determined to find them. My good friend Mark Lehner and I spent several seasons carrying out various projects on the plateau, but the first great discovery, the cemetery of the pyramid builders, was made by chance (although in the general area where I was certain there were important remains). On one hot August day in 1990 an American tourist was riding in the desert south of the Wall of the Crow when her horse stumbled on an ancient mud-brick wall and threw her. The chief guard at Giza came to fetch me, and I hurried to the site of the accident. The tourist was fine, and the mud-brick wall turned out to be part of an Old Kingdom tomb belonging to an over-seer named Ptah-shepsesu.

This turned out to be only the first of hundreds of tombs that cover the flanks of the low desert south of the Wall of the Crow. There are two distinct cemeteries: the first, which lies on the low desert, contains a number of large tombs belonging to overseers, each surrounded by a number of much smaller tombs for the workmen he supervised and his family. Above this, on the slope leading up to the higher plateau, are larger, more elaborate tombs, some with exquisite decoration obviously provided by the royal workshops, where minor officials and artisans were buried. Thus these men and women, far from being slaves, were granted the honor of burial in the shadow of the masters they had served in life.

The workmen's tombs come in many sizes and styles, and probably represent a number of regional traditions brought to the capital by workers conscripted from the provinces. Long vaulted galleries stand be-side simple rectangular mastabas, in some cases reduced to a low mud platform, a little over a meter (three feet) long and about thirty centimeters (twelve inches) high. Prominently featured are the tiny niches on the east faces that served as false doors and which were the focus for the offering ritual. One overseer built his tomb in the form of a stepped pyramid, and several other pyramids and dome-shaped tombs have been found in the pyramid builders' cemetery. Thus we know that in the Old Kingdom the pyramidal shape, representing the primeval mound and a stairway to the sky, was not, as was believed until now, restricted to royal use only but was part of the common repertoire. Perhaps only workers laboring in the service of the pyramid-building kings could use such a shape, or perhaps the shape itself was borrowed by the kings themselves from some long-standing folk tradition.

Mud brick is used extensively in these monuments, but so are crude pieces of limestone, granite, basalt, and quartzite set in mud mortar. These stones are all debris from the construction of the nearby pyramids and elite tombs, discarded fragments of fine stones that the humbler people gathered for use in their own monuments.

The more elaborate tombs higher up on the hillside are generally either cut into the rock, with a limestone facade against the cliff face, or built of quarried limestone blocks. A ramp links the lower and upper cemeteries. A large, impressive beehive tomb, the local variant of the pyramid form and eerily reminiscent of a modern sheikh's tomb, stands prominently at the top of this ramp.

We found wonderful artifacts in these tombs, from pottery vessels to tools. A number of burials included offering tables bearing the names and titles of the tomb owner. Much to our surprise, we also found a number of small, well-crafted statues, demonstrating that their owners were able to command the work of skilled sculptors, perhaps from among their own community.

In 1991 one of my best inspectors, Mansour Boriak, was supervising excavations in the pyramid builders' cemetery when he saw a backhoe, which was working in the low desert directly to the east, expose a stratum of Old Kingdom pottery. We stopped the clearance immediately, since it was obvious that an important site lay just below the surface. Mark Lehner had planned a season at Giza, and began work in this area. He immediately hit an Old Kingdom bakery; in subsequent seasons he has uncovered a vast royal installation, where the workmen were housed, fed, and equipped. He has also discovered houses belonging to some of the supervisors and perhaps some of the artisans and minor officials buried in the upper cemetery. This area seems to date to the reigns of Khafre and especially Menkaure. It is possible that Khufu's installation lay beneath and was built over by his successors, or, as suggested above, that a similar installation was once located here or elsewhere on the plateau and razed after the king died and his immediate successor moved to Abu Rawash.

The royal installation is surrounded by walls of fieldstone, which enclose an area whose boundaries have not yet been completely defined. A road runs through a monumental doorway in the Wall of the Crow, along the west side of the installation, and then through a gateway in the installation wall. Within the installation, the central buildings are organized along wide east–west streets, with what look like control buildings at either end. The temporary workmen from the provinces, and local farmers who would have come to Giza during the workweek and returned home for the weekend, were housed in long galleries containing mud-brick sleeping platforms fronting on these streets. Each gallery could have slept forty to fifty workmen; the entire site could have housed up to two thousand men at a time. The town in which the supervisors and artisans lived is at the eastern edge of the site and continues into the floodplain, where it disappears beneath the village of Nazlet el-Samman—thirty-six houses of overseers have been found to date.

Adjacent to the galleries on the east was a hypostyle, or pillared, hall, one of the earliest examples known in Egypt. Running through the hall are a series of low mud-brick benches, and found embedded in the mud brick were numerous fish bones. This was most likely a dining hall, where the workmen took many of their meals. The same system is still in place in Egypt today: when the government has a project such as a dam, the workmen sleep on the site and eat in one place under government supervision. Just as in the ancient past, much of the food for these modern work projects comes from the households that provide the manpower.

The installation area at Giza included numerous bakeries, workshops, and a large building that contained granaries and other storage facilities. An enormous quantity of food would have been necessary to feed the workforce. Bread, as attested by the countless bread molds found all over the site, was the principal staple of the workers' diet, and beer was the primary beverage. In addition to bread and beer, the workers were given garlic and onions. Perhaps daily (for example, for lunch), judging from the density of the fish bones littered in the hypostyle hall, they ate fish caught in the nearby Nile. The most popular fish at Giza was the bolti; in one excavation square in the same general area, a bronze fish hook, similar in shape to a type still in use today, was found.

One of the biggest surprises to emerge from recent excavations in the royal installation is that the workmen ate a lot of meat, probably every day. It has long been assumed that only the elite ate meat in any quantity, but the vast number of bones found in the workmen's area at Giza suggests that eleven cattle and thirty-three sheep and goats were slaughtered each day, enough to feed ten thousand workmen (a reasonable estimate of the number of workers on the site). Consistent with most animal husbandry, only male cattle were killed, since the females would have been kept to bear young. It is likely that these cattle, sheep, and goats were not raised at Giza but were brought to the site. There are two possible sources for this livestock. One was the king's estates, which might have sent meat daily to the site. We know from a text dated to the reign of Khafre that at one point, his pyramid and temples owned 1,055 cattle, 974 goats, and 2,235 sheep. Another possible source was the tens of thousands of households all over Egypt, which might have been responsible for sending meat to the pyramid project once a month. We know from textual sources, for example, that the nome of Kom el-Hissan, in the Delta, raised cattle. But recent excavations in Old Kingdom strata here have found only the bones of pigs and sheep, suggesting that all the cattle were sent to Giza to feed the workmen.

Bread and beer were important staples of the Egyptian diet. There were several large buildings in the royal installation designed to store grain, and we expect to discover more evidence for grinding grain. There were numerous bakeries on the site, and bread molds—thick, rough clay vessels in which the dough was baked—are scattered all over the site.

Pottery vessels imported from Palestine have also been found on the site. These were used to transport and store olive oil. This type of ware, called combed ware, had been found earlier at Giza by George Reisner.

We know a little bit about the organization of the provinces from which food and materials would have been sent to Giza. Upper Egypt was divided into twenty-two nomes; Lower Egypt contained twenty nomes. Within each nome were fields dedicated to agriculture, villages, and estates owned by absentee landowners such as the crown or the temples. Each nome was governed by a nomarch. Each town or village was headed by a mayor. There would also have been a number of "sheikhs," or heads of extended families, within each town. In the reign of Khufu, the title *adj-mer* ("canal cutter") appeared as an important title. Each nome also had administrators called *imi-ra* ("overseer"), who could also act as the chief priests of the town temples. The nome administration, headed by one or two dominant households, appears to have taken responsibility for collecting the harvest tax and sending it to the royal house, distant temples, and anyone else who had a claim to land within the territory of the nome.

The permanent building and support staff would have lived in the village southeast of the pyramids. An example of the type of house that would have been inhabited by an overseer or official of comparable rank was excavated in the mid-twentieth century just south of Menkaure's causeway. It consists of several rooms for sleeping and a courtyard for cooking, including an oven. Other examples of larger permanent houses have been excavated recently by Mark Lehner just east of the pyramid builders' cemetery. The village of the artisans at Giza shows that each artisan, draftsman, craftsman, and sculptor lived in a house consisting of a room to store his materials and a court for his work in the daylight; attached to this area would be rooms for sleeping, reception areas for meeting people, kitchens for the preparation of food, and storage areas.

The royal installation provides a unique glimpse into the highly developed ancient Egyptian bureaucracy. Every man, woman, and child was accounted for, and each item of food and clothing was recorded. We even know, from records at the New Kingdom site of Deir el-Medineh, that the workers' tools were carefully tracked. At Giza, an administrative center (a pillared building near the paved road) would have been the central distribution point for the food consumed by the workmen. It is likely that the storage place for the tools, checked in and out by the individual workers each day, was located near this building.

Chapter Eighteen

The Lives of the Pyramid Builders

It was hot in the quarry, the sun blazing down on the toiling men. But the quarrymen were hardened and worked steadily despite the heat. Each group sang a work song, praising the king and their own prowess. The men of Green, proud members of the Friends of Khufu, were from Upper Egypt. They had tools of diorite, flint, and granite, with which they cut deep channels in the stone. Other workmen smoothed the sides of the stone, polishing them with diorite pounders. Once the stones were cut, the overseer called on the men of the Prow to bring the sledges and ropes, load up the stones, and drag them, chanting as they labored, up the ramp to the pyramid rising in the distance.

The overseer Khenmu, a cheerful, hardworking man who had recently been promoted to the position of director of building tombs, noticed that one of his men was holding his head again. He always seemed to have a headache, and today it looked especially severe. Khenmu was concerned. He approached the suffering workman, who suddenly cried out and fell to the ground. Khenmu sent his assistant to fetch the emergency medical team and ordered the other men to move *their comrade into the shade and then keep working—they couldn't afford to lose*

another minute if they were to keep on schedule. The nurses came quickly from

their station to the south of the pyramid, accompanied by two men with a litter.

They loaded the fallen man onto the litter and carried him to the clinic, holding a

cloth above his head to shield him from the burning sun. The physician on duty

examined him and found that he had cancer and would need surgery. The operation

took many hours, but it was successful, and he lived for two more years, although he

never went back to the quarry.

*T*he discoveries in the cemetery of the pyramid builders have introduced us to many of the individual men and women who helped to
build the great monuments at Giza, and the discovery of the royal installation has given us a great deal of information about the day-to-day lives
of these people.

We know, for example, of a man named Itysen, who was an overseer
of the king's work, in charge of one side of the pyramid. He would have
monitored the stones brought to build his side of the structure, made
sure they were transported properly and placed safely and efficiently. We
know of another man whose title was overseer of the west side of the
pyramid, although we do not know his name. Senmeru was in charge of
the blocks of white limestone that came from Tura and the rosy granite
from Aswan to be used in the pyramid casing. Another overseer, named
Merer, was in charge of a phyle and would have supervised the work of
his gang, making sure they were properly fed and drank enough water
over the course of the day, overseeing their travel to and from the work
site, and monitoring their sleeping arrangements, perhaps within the
large dormitories. The supervisors themselves would have lived with
their families in the nearby houses.

Wenemniut would have supervised the offerings sent from the royal farms, making sure that enough grain and cattle were delivered each week. Nyankhptah was the chief baker and would have supervised the grain being taken from the granaries to the bakeries and baked into the thousands of loaves of bread needed to feed the huge workforce. Another official would have been in charge of butchering the cattle, cooking the meat, and making sure that each workman got his daily share of about two hundred to three hundred grams. Wahy, an inspector of the washers, would have made sure that the workmen had clean linen to wear.

Among the tombs in the upper cemetery is a limestone mastaba belonging to a man named Nefertheith and his two wives. The tomb chapel consists of a long hallway with three false doors and an offering and festival list set into the western wall. Each wife, along with her children, was honored on her own false door; and the first wife, Nyankhhathor, who had evidently died before the doors were carved, was mourned here by her husband. The couple had seven children; it is tempting to hypothesize that she died in childbirth, probably the most common cause of death among women until only recently. The second wife, Neferhetepes, bore an unusual title that has been interpreted as "midwife": she would have had plenty of practice at home, since she appears to have had eleven children of her own! She is shown as her husband's equal within the tomb, drawn at the same scale.

Nefertheith himself bore the title of chief baker; the decoration of two of his false doors has been planned accordingly: small vignettes at the bottom of the northernmost and southernmost false doors depict the making of bread and beer. On the left side a woman is straining the mash through a sieve while a man pours the beer into jars. Both the man and woman are unnamed. On the right side a kneeling woman called Khenut is grinding grain on a saddle quern, and facing her a man named Kakai-ankh stokes the fire under a pile of bread molds while shading his face from the heat with his hand.

On the inner panels of the false door of Nefertheith, he and Neferhetepes stand facing each other accompanied by their sons. Beneath them are two men identified as *ka* priests carrying baskets of food. The scenes of food preparation and *ka* priests bringing provisions were undoubtedly intended to ensure a constant supply of offerings, like scenes of food production in the elite tomb chapels of this time. However, the addition of these small scenes of brewing and baking to the standard false door and their position underneath the figures of the tomb owners is extremely unusual. An important detail for dating this tomb is the name of the baker, Kakai-ankh, which is based on the name of Neferirkare-Kakai, the third king of the 5th Dynasty. This indicates that Nefertheith and his wife probably lived during his reign or just after.

In contrast to the representations of Nefertheith and his wives, another official buried in the upper cemetery, Pettety, and his wife, Nesy-Sokar, are only depicted separately. She was a priestess of the goddess Hathor, lady of the sycomore, and is described as "beloved of the goddess Neith." One scene shows Nesy-Sokar and a daughter who holds a mirror and a bag. The reliefs of Nesy-Sokar are bold and striking. She is shown standing on the doorjamb of the chapel in a traditional pose with one arm raised to her breast and the other behind her back. The artist has portrayed her with her head slightly tilted up and forward, perhaps a realistic touch caused by the fact that she is wearing a wide, tight collar around her neck. This gives her face a bold and confident expression enhanced by the darkly outlined eye.

Another measure of her independence is suggested by a unique curse that occurs in two variants, one beside her figure and the other beside that of her husband:

O anyone who enters this tomb,
Who will make evil against this tomb:
May the crocodile be against him on water,
And the snake against him on land.

May the hippopotamus be against him on water,
The scorpion against him on land.

Pettety's curse is much the same as his wife's, except that he calls on the crocodile, lion, and hippopotamus.

The majority of women's graves were joint burials with their husbands. Two women, however, were found in their own tombs. One of them is named Repyt-Hathor on the small offering basin placed in front of her false door; this also bore a title identifying her as a priestess of Hathor. The second was a priestess of the goddess Neith named Nubi, whose tomb was considerably grander than that of Repyt-Hathor.

One family is represented by a group of three small statues discovered in a tiny box formed of three limestone slabs, found in association with a miniature mastaba tomb for the burial of a man named Kaihep and his wife Hepnikawes. The husband is represented as a standing figure wearing a kilt, while his lady is shown seated on a stool, wearing the long, tight white dress typical of the Old Kingdom. The third small statue found depicts a kneeling woman grinding flour. This is a type of servant figure of which several examples are known from 5th Dynasty tombs at Giza and Saqqara. It is carefully made and remarkably well preserved. The woman wears a short white dress and has black hair, and the sculptor has suggested the strength in her shoulders and the action of the grinding by depicting her right arm as slightly longer than her left. The quern is slanted slightly forward. It is painted red in imitation of quartzite, with a white patch in the center to indicate the flour. Between her knees the woman has a small bag that probably contained the grain.

In contrast to the statues of Kaihep and Hepnikawes, this piece is uninscribed, and thus leaves open an interesting debate about the role of such statues and the lifestyle of the people buried in these tombs. We do not know whether these laborers had servants of their own, or if, as government employees, they were supplied by the state with servants to do such menial tasks. Does this figure of a woman grinding depict Hepnikawes' servant or is this a chore that Hepnikawes would have had to do herself? In the second case, the figure may represent Hepnikawes. Or perhaps its presence is merely an indication of the owner's hopes for servants and a better existence in the afterlife. Whatever the correct interpretation, this group provides a fascinating window into family life among the lower classes at Giza.

The physically stressful lives led by the men and women buried in this cemetery can be read in their bones. In comparison to the members of the elite class buried on the main plateau, who had an average life span of fifty to sixty years, the pyramid builders lived significantly shorter life spans, with a life expectancy of thirty-five to forty years. For people under the age of thirty, females had a higher mortality rate than males, undoubtedly reflecting the hazards of childbirth. Among the older age groups the mortality of females is highest between the ages of thirty-five and thirty-nine. On the whole, the working men and women, again in comparison to their wealthier contemporaries, were of relatively short stature.

Degenerative joint diseases were common among the artisans and workers and more severe than in the upper-class skeletons of the elite cemeteries. These diseases, which are caused primarily by physical stress, were found especially in the vertebral column, in particular in the lumbar region, and in the knees. This implies a vigorous lifestyle for the artisans and workers, which may be the main cause of the degenerative arthritis found among them. Fractures of the cranium and extremities were frequent, perhaps attesting to the dangerous nature of their work. Depressed fractures of the parietal bone were found in two female skulls. Both were on the left side, indicating that the injuries were the result of face-to-face assaults by right-handed attackers. Extremity fractures were found in both the artisans and workers, and there were skeletons that showed healing and therefore survival after fracturing. One male had one leg that had been successfully amputated; he lived for several years after the accident. Another workman had had brain surgery.

Two especially interesting burials were that of a dwarf woman, little more than one meter (three feet) in height, who had apparently died in childbirth. The skeleton of her baby was found inside its mother's body. Another is that of a young lady approximately fifteen years old who was buried holding a shell kohl pot in her hand. Kohl was used to line the eyes and has medicinal properties that protect them from infection. It was also associated with ritual purity and divine qualities, which are reflected in the heavily outlined eyes of statues and reliefs.

In addition to the workers and supervisors stationed at Giza, the pyramid project, as I have explained, required expeditions to quarries and mines at places such as Aswan (granite); Nubia (hard stone such as diorite); Tura and Bahariya Oasis (fine limestone); Hatnub (alabaster); and Sinai (for exotic stones and precious metals). The quarrymen sent to foreign locales would have been drawn from the same social strata as the Giza workers, so the information we are gaining at Giza applies equally well to these men. The local quarries, such as the workings at Tura, could have been manned by local farmers and provincial conscripts. However, expeditions to farther-off locales, such as the Sinai mines or the Toshka diorite quarries, required specially trained workers. Goods from even more exotic locations—such as incense from Punt, located between Ethiopia and Sudan on the coast of the Red Sea; silver from Syro-Palestine; and lapis lazuli from Afghanistan—would have been brought via trading caravans. Both trading caravans and quarrying missions that took place outside the boundaries of Egypt were dangerous, and soldiers were necessary to safeguard the expeditions.

Our information about quarrying and mining in the Old Kingdom comes from scenes found in the royal pyramid complexes, scenes and inscriptions found near the quarries and mines themselves or on the roads leading to these sites, and from biographies of private individuals who participated in the expeditions. The textual sources give us information about the number of workmen and soldiers participating, and even, in some cases, the date of a particular mission.

Each expedition was led by an overseer of the royal work, a royal sealer, and a priest; also necessary were scribes and, of course, the workers and soldiers themselves. Inscriptions from the alabaster quarry at Hatnub tell us that the number of workmen needed to cut the stone varied from three to sixteen hundred. These workers and their bodyguards would have lived in temporary huts. The equipment necessary for quarrying included tools for cutting the stones, large wooden levers to detach the blocks, sledges for moving the cut blocks, and boats for transporting them back to Giza. An average team at Tura might have moved about 340 blocks during ten hours of work.

I would like to end this section with an overview of the lives of the Giza workmen, based on the evidence that scholars have collected and analyzed over the years, with the addition of the new information we are finding at Giza.

The pyramid workers rose before sunrise (perhaps wakened by a drummer) and labored until sunset, about ten hours a day. They ate, as we have seen, significant amounts of meat, supplemented by bread, garlic, and onions—without animal protein, they would have been unable to function well enough to move heavy stones day in and day out. Breakfast and lunch were probably brought to them at the site by support staff, which would have included women. Also important would have been the water supply, brought by donkeys in large pottery jars.

The workmen, as we have discussed, were carefully organized into phyles and then into gangs. Some went to the pyramid quarry to pry the bedrock from the mother stone, pounding away with granite, diorite, and other hard stones. The techniques of quarrying stone were highly developed by this point; and the quarrymen worked quickly, probably producing somewhere in the region of 300 to 350 stones of various sizes a day. Other gangs moved the stones from the quarry to the ramp, and still others moved the stones up the ramp to the pyramid itself. Specific gangs were assigned to each face of the pyramid. The workers would have sung or chanted as they work, as workmen still do in Egypt today.

At sunset, a drum would signal that work was finished, and the workers would stop their toil, happy to go back to the installation to clean up and have a dinner of grilled meat or fish, bread, and beer in the communal dining hall. All this must have been very organized, and the workmen would have followed strict discipline, or there would have been chaos.

After an exhausting day of cutting and hauling stones, the workmen now, as today, would have headed early to bed. A few particularly energetic fellows might have gone to the green marshes or the desert, or perhaps headed off to meet a girlfriend or gather with a group to hear a flute, harp, or drum player. Perhaps some nights, musicians or professional dancers were sent by the palace to amuse the pyramid builders.

The workers took one day off in every ten. In addition, we know of numerous feast days, which would also have been holidays for the workers. The workers who lived near the pyramid site would have gone home (probably setting out the night before) to see their wives, children, or girlfriends and clean their clothes. Those from far-flung nomes might have had a party the night before, with singing and dancing and perhaps a dwarf for entertainment. On the day of the holiday, they perhaps would have gone with a party of friends or a girlfriend for a boat ride on the Nile.

In addition to the one day off every ten days, the pyramid builders would have celebrated the numerous holidays marked by the Egyptians: the feast of Djehuty, the feast of the half-moon, the feast of the full moon, the feast of Re, the feast of the beginning of the new year, and the feast of the harvest, to name a few. There would also have been festivals for the pyramid building itself, such as the first day of the foundation of the pyramid and the feast of the completion of the pyramid. We think that the Egyptians had as many as one hundred feasts a year, although it is unlikely that the Giza workmen celebrated anywhere near all of these.

The artisans, as men of higher rank, would have followed a similar but much less grueling schedule. They lived with their families in larger, more comfortable houses, organized around courtyards. They would have spent most of their time in their workshops, producing the exquisite art that graced the pyramid complexes. Some were draftsmen, sketching the images to be carved onto the walls of the temples. There would have been a master draftsman, responsible for organizing the work and making corrections, and many lower-ranking artisans to do the actual sketching, most likely from pattern books of some sort. Then the sculptors would have come along and carved the images into the stone; and finally, the painters would have added the color. Other sculptors and painters would have carved and colored the royal statues in the round found in the complexes of Khafre and Menkaure, and the private statues found in elite tombs from these reigns.

Another group of artisans would have produced the furniture and other items to be used by the king and his family in their afterlives. Others would have been responsible for preparing for, and eventually carrying out, the mummification of the king's body; they would presumably also have dealt with the preparation of the bodies of high-ranking noblemen and -women.

We return now to the royal family and the decline of the 4th Dynasty. The lives of the common people—the pyramid builders and their far-flung families, the peasants who tilled the fields and worked the quarries—probably went on much as usual, little affected by the fortunes of the royal family. But great changes were afoot on high, changes that would finally bring down the house of Sneferu and Khufu and leave a new dynasty, men loyal above all to the cult of the sun god Re at Heliopolis, on the throne of the Two Lands.

Part Five

The End
of an Era

Chapter Nineteen

Shepseskaf, the Good Son

T he Saqqara king list mentions four names after Menkaure, and the Turin Canon mentions three. However, it is the succession outlined in the Abydos list that is generally taken as correct by Egyptologists. In this list, Menkaure is followed by a short-lived king named Shepseskaf, usually assumed to be his son.

One of the few aspects of the royal succession that we know for certain is that the crown prince was responsible for the funeral of his father. By carrying out the proper burial rites, the new king took on the role of Horus, who, in Egyptian mythology, was responsible for the burial of his father. We have seen this already at the end of Khufu's reign, when the great king's son and successor, Djedefre, performed his funeral rites. As evidence of his piety, he left his own name inscribed on the blocks covering the pits holding dismantled wooden boats to the south of the Great Pyramid.

Menkaure died after eighteen years of rule, leaving his pyramid complex far from complete. It is generally held that his presumed son and successor, Shepseskaf, finished his father's monument. However, he either did not have, or chose not to commit, the resources necessary to complete the complex in the style in which it had been planned. He did not finish smoothing the granite casing that covered the lowest sixteen

courses of the pyramid, and, rather than completing his father's monumental temples in stone, he used mud brick. The clearest evidence that
this work was carried out by Shepseskaf is in the form of a fragmentary
text found in Menkaure's mortuary temple, part of which bears the
name of Shepseskaf. Another fragment reads: "He made it as a monument for his father, the king of Upper and Lower Egypt, Menkaure." In
this temple, a niche was cut into the northern wall of the entrance; a
matching niche may have been cut into the southern wall. Reisner believed that the fragments of this text come from a pair of steles placed
by Shepseskaf, dedicating his father's temple. Shepseskaf also made the
open court of the temple level, using mud and debris, and then paved it
with limestone slabs. In the debris filling the temple portico, Reisner's
team found fragments of two steles dated to the reign of Shepseskaf and
two decrees in limestone, one bearing the Horus name of Merenre of
the 6th Dynasty.

Shepseskaf himself ruled for only four years. He chose as the site
of his own mortuary monument Saqqara, where Djoser had long ago
built his Step Pyramid. Instead of a pyramid, Shepseskaf built a huge
mastaba of stone, one hundred meters (328 feet) long, seventy-two meters (236 feet) wide, and eighteen meters (fifty-nine feet) high, with a
causeway and temple in mud brick. The mastaba is in the form of a giant sarcophagus, with rectangular sides and an arched roof.

Like the pyramids of his forebears, Shepseskaf's mastaba represents
the primeval mound on which the creator god stood to bring the cosmos into being. However, his tomb does not carry the blatantly solar
overtones of the true pyramids, and scholars have questioned his relationship to the cult of the sun god. The fact that his name was not compounded with the name of Re is also evidence for a distancing from this
dogma. On the other hand, some scholars suggest that at least one example of his name, found in his causeway, should be read Shepseskare,
and he did bear the title Son of Re. It may be simply that he did not have
the wealth needed to build a pyramid. He seems to have continued with

the political systems of his father and in most ways continued the traditions of his 4th Dynasty predecessors. In addition to finishing his father's complex, he honored Menkaure's cult by exempting the priests of the temples from paying taxes.

In other ways, Shepseskaf did break with ancient tradition. He married his daughter to a man, Shepsesptah, who was not of royal blood but lived at the palace of Menkaure. This was the first time in pharaonic history that we know of a royal princess marrying a commoner.

Recently, an Egyptologist named Peter Janosi, who studied the subsidiary pyramids at Giza, questioned whether Shepseskaf, in his short reign of four years, could have finished so many elements of the Menkaure complex when he had his own giant stone mastaba to build, along with its temple and causeway in mud brick. It is true that the archaeological and textual records of the pyramids do not include clear instances of such extensive work carried out by kings on the complexes of other kings.

If it was not Shepseskaf, who took the responsibility for finishing off Menkaure's monuments and creating a functioning pyramid complex? Could the builders have turned to mud brick already in Menkaure's reign? Or was some of the work done under Khentkawes, a mysterious female monarch who declared in her own colossal monument at Giza that she was the mother of either one or two kings of Upper and Lower Egypt? Her titles may imply that she ruled Egypt as king in her own right at the end of the Giza dynasty, so it is to this elusive queen that we next turn our attention.

Chapter Twenty

The Rising of the Sons of Re

The Reign of Khentkawes and the Dawn of the 5th Dynasty

A massive monument, in the shape of a giant square sarcophagus on a high podium like that of Shepseskaf, still stands at the south of the Giza plateau between the causeways of Khafre and Menkaure. The base of the tomb, which was cut into the solid rock and cased with fine white limestone, measures forty-five meters (148 feet), and its original height was forty-five meters (148 feet). The size and square base of this tomb prompted its main excavator, Selim Hassan, to christen it the "fourth Giza pyramid." Under the tomb is a burial chamber lined with granite and containing a false door, along with seven small rooms designed to house furniture to be used in the afterlife.

A small mortuary temple stands against the eastern face of this structure, and a causeway leads to a valley temple. The mortuary temple was cased with granite and decorated with religious scenes. On the southwest side of the tomb, Hassan found a boat pit cut into the rock; matching this to the northeast is a rectangular pool entered by eleven steps.

This tomb is dedicated to a queen named Khentkawes, who was a daughter of the god and also claimed a title that can be read as either "king's mother and king of Upper and Lower Egypt" or "mother of two kings of Upper and Lower Egypt." Thus she may have been a ruling queen, the last monarch of the 4th Dynasty. She was certainly a princess; although her parentage is technically unknown, it is most likely that she was the daughter of Menkaure and the sister and wife of Shepseskaf, giving her multiple claims to the throne in the absence of a strong male heir.

As a woman, Khentkawes would not technically have had the right to hold the throne of Egypt, and, not surprisingly, her name does not appear in any of the later king lists. However, her clearly royal monument and her title suggest strongly that however ephemerally, she sat on the throne of the Two Lands. One image of the queen in her tomb, recently examined by Czech Egyptologist Miroslav Verner, shows her wearing a uraeus cobra on her brow, normally seen only on kings during this period. Within her valley temple, a small pyramid city thrived, demonstrating that her cult was active for a significant period of time and providing further evidence that she was accepted as a ruler of Egypt.

Some scholars believe that Khentkawes was the mother of Userkaf, first ruler of the 5th Dynasty, and thus provides a link between the end of the 4th Dynasty and the beginning of the 5th. It has also been theorized that Khentkawes married a priest of Heliopolis and that her children and the heirs to the throne were only half royal.

Userkaf moved the royal court to the site of Abusir, where he built a relatively small pyramid complex. The pyramids of the 5th Dynasty kings were smaller in size than their 4th Dynasty precursors but were more impressive in terms of the areas covered by beautiful relief decoration. In addition to their own mortuary complexes, each king built a sun temple, a monument to Re. These temples, of which only two have been found and excavated, are nearby and are laid out like the pyramid complexes. The major difference is that, instead of a pyramid, the complexes held monumental obelisks—tapering rectangular shafts that end with a pyramid-shaped top. These sun temples provide strong evidence that the relationship of the royal house to the priesthood of Re had undergone a major shift. The deceased sun god was seen as separate from the deceased king, and thus needed his own mortuary temple.

In the late 1970s, Verner found a pyramid that he believed to belong to a queen named Khentkawes, who was given the same title as the Giza Khentkawes, perhaps in this case to be read "mother of two kings of Upper and Lower Egypt." Verner identifies this woman as Khentkawes II and suggests that she was the wife of Neferirkare-Kakai and the mother of Neferefre and Niuserre, and thus lived in the middle of the 5th Dynasty. Other scholars want to identify this woman as Khentkawes I, and suggest that the queen mother moved to Abusir with her children. I think it more likely, especially given the Egyptian propensity for handing down both names and titles, that there were two important queens named Khentkawes.

Texts in several tombs at Giza indicate that there was no dramatic political break between the 4th and 5th Dynasties. One of Khafre's sons, Sekhemkare, recorded in his tomb that kings Khafre, Menkaure, Shepseskaf, Userkaf, and Sahure all paid him honor. An official named Neferpunesut was in royal favor from the reigns of Djedefre to Sahure, while Ptahshepses, high priest of Ptah under Niuserre, was brought up in the households of Menkaure and Shepseskaf. We must remember that the whole concept of dynasties is a later construct, that the Egyptians themselves saw their kings in an unbroken line. However, there must have been some change of family, and the anomalous rule of Queen Khentkawes I provides evidence of difficulties with the succession.

Chapter Twenty-one

The Abandonment of Giza

With the death of Queen Khentkawes, the glory days of Giza were over. The 5th Dynasty court moved south, to the site of Abusir. The cults of the Giza kings continued, although they were no longer the focus of the nation's pride and the primary consumer of its resources.

Priests of Khufu, Khafre, and Menkaure are known from the 4th Dynasty to the end of the 6th Dynasty; thus the Giza kings were still honored and their cults maintained through the entire Old Kingdom. Over time, some of the agricultural assets that had been committed to these cults were reallocated. In the 6th Dynasty, tomb texts mention only forty-eight of the known estates of Khufu, and only one of the fifty-one estates of Khafre is securely attested for this period. But high-ranking officials continued to be buried in the Giza cemeteries until the end of the Old Kingdom, though the court had moved away.

We know, for example, that the cult of Khufu continued until the First Intermediate Period, and we know of about 115 people connected with Khufu's cult during this era. They would have been supported in part by estates set up by Khufu and Hemiunu, dedicated to the maintenance of the king's cult. Most priests of royal cults served more than one king, so they would gain additional support from other royal estates. These positions were inherited.

Most of Khufu's priests were buried at Giza, but some 5th and 6th dynasty individuals were buried at Saqqara, Abusir, or Sheikh Said. The seven individuals not buried at Giza must have inherited their titles and been more involved with the cults of other kings, their association with the cults of the Giza kings being secondary. For example, a man named Ptahmerseti, whose tomb is at Abusir, was in charge of the *ka* priests of Queen Khentkawes and overseer of the pyramid of Neferirkare at Abusir. Seferka, who was buried at Sheik Said (perhaps his birthplace) was priest of both Khufu and Userkaf of the 5th Dynasty. Of the five people attested at Saqqara, two were officials of the cults of Sahure and Niuserre, two may have been buried at Saqqara for family reasons, and the lintel on which the name of the fifth was found may have originally stood in a tomb at Giza.

Menkaure's valley temple provides archaeological evidence for the ongoing cults of the Giza kings and also paints a picture for us of the actual, rather than the ideal, life of a pyramid cult. Although the king's name continued to be honored, his monuments did not fare quite as well. For example, within a century of Menkaure's funeral, the residents of the village sprawled around his temple smashed some of the royal statues to make model vessels for use in contemporary tombs. Before the temple was abandoned after a flash flood, the people charged with maintaining Menkaure's memorial service, who were clearly very poor, plundered the magazines. The evidence for this lies strewn about the floor of the court. In the later phase of the temple town, the residents were still smashing statues, but they were also careful to preserve the raison d'être of their habitation—the temple sanctuary.

What kind of people were these temple townsfolk? Were the same kinds of communities growing up around the valley temples of Khufu and Khafre? In a decree of Pepi I found at Dahshur, the residents of Sneferu's pyramid town are called *khentiu-she*, literally "those in front of the basin/precinct." They include people of various occupations in specific types of service to the household of the deceased king. The decree frees residents from conscript labor and exempts their trees, canals, and wells from taxation. It was found in front of an enclosure that could be the walled town of the Sneferu valley complex; current excavations by a German team may add to our understanding of this type of settlement.

How many lived in the town associated with the Menkaure valley temple? The organic way in which the settlement grew, combined with the fact that the original exploration of this area took place at the dawn of scientific archaeology—before the techniques of detailed, stratigraphic excavation had been refined—make it difficult to reconstruct the different phases of occupation accurately. However, it is possible to see at least three phases of construction. The basic organization seems to be houses to the south and granaries to the north; there might have been between six and ten small houses or so in each period. With four or five people per house, the population within the temple walls would have been forty to fifty people. It is also possible, however, that these houses were not the principal residences of these priestly families but a way of staking claim to the benefits earned through the right to carry out the royal cult. The town associated with the valley temple of Khentkawes is larger than Menkaure's town, with more than a dozen larger, well-planned houses.

Thus even though the royal cults continued, robbing the monuments at Giza began during the later Old Kingdom, probably as early as the 5th Dynasty. The mastaba cemeteries east and west of the Great Pyramid sanded up quickly at the end of the 6th Dynasty, but Reisner saw evidence that prior to this there was plundering being carried out systematically while the streets were filled with only a little sand. Some of this may have taken place as early as the 5th Dynasty, when the cults of the kings were still operational. Structures attached to some of the mastabas of cemetery GI-S, the mastaba row south of the Khufu pyramid, were being used during this period as makeshift workshops to hack up statues of Khafre for making stone implements and vessels. The excavator theorized that the plunderers broke up the statues in the Khafre pyramid temple, then under the cover of darkness brought the pieces to cemetery GI-S for recarving into alabaster model vessels to be used as burial equipment.

Smashing royal statues and plundering mastaba tombs are small-scale acts that individuals or small local groups could have carried out during times of slackening control. This vandalism might have been possible because the royal house and necropolis had moved to Abusir and Saqqara.

In the 6th Dynasty, there is evidence in Menkaure's complex of a certain amount of pious attention. Although his statues continued to be broken up for making model vessels, the 6th Dynasty priests of Menkaure responsible for rebuilding his valley temple and reinstating his cult clearly favored him over his father: the entrance door into the vestibule of the town in front of Menkaure's valley temple turned on a pivot socket carved into the left foot of a broken diorite statue of Khafre inscribed with his Horus and cartouche names.

This continuity of cult service alongside the reuse of ancient elements continued throughout the 5th and 6th Dynasties. Though the kings were building their pyramids at Abusir and Saqqara, those involved with the Giza cults continued to be buried near their ancient masters, fitting their tombs between the older monuments within the ancient cites of the dead. Since priesthood was in general hereditary, it is likely that the later burials were made near the tombs of their 4th Dynasty forebears.

After end of the 6th Dynasty, the Old Kingdom quickly declined, and the chaos of the First Intermediate Period, when warring local princes fought for control of Egypt, ensued. There is evidence, as mentioned above, of vandalism and violence at Giza during the First Intermediate Period, as if by destroying the Giza monuments the memory of a hated era could be erased. Later offering places and burials intruded into the sand fill and mastaba cores of the Giza cemeteries. According to Reisner, these intrusive burials were later than the 6th Dynasty, but earlier than the 12th Dynasty, so were made either in the late Old Kingdom or during the First Intermediate Period. A literary tradition, developed later, after the country had been reunited by the Middle Kingdom dynasts, decried the disrespect with which ancient monuments were treated during the years of chaos, providing textual support for the archaeological evidence of destruction during this period.

The plateau then stood mostly still and abandoned for almost six hundred years, through the renaissance of the Middle Kingdom and the foreign invasions of the Second Intermediate Period, until the dawn of the New Kingdom. The first king of the 12th Dynasty, Amenemhet I (c. 1991–1962 B.C.), did take some of the fallen fragments of relief to use as fill in his own pyramid at Lisht, as if to identify himself with the noble past. Blocks belonging to Khufu probably came from his pyramid and valley temples, and part of a red granite architrave bearing the names of Khafre most likely derived from that king's mortuary temple.

However, these reused pieces do not suggest that Amenemhet I systematically plundered the royal monuments for raw material for his Lisht pyramid, at least from what has been documented so far. It rather suggests a picking up of odds and ends with royal inscriptions from several sites (fragments from the complexes of several later Old Kingdom kings also were found in his pyramid fill), probably from monuments already vandalized. In any event, the Middle Kingdom rulers left few footprints behind them at Giza: only one small statue and one statuette from somewhere around the Sphinx have been dated to this period. Although interest in the Giza kings was high during the entire Middle Kingdom and Second Intermediate Period, as attested by texts such as the Westcar Papyrus and the Wadi Hammamat inscription, no one carried out cult activity in any of the Giza temples; the cemeteries were abandoned, and no one undertook new construction.

The New Kingdom saw a return of both piety and plundering to the Giza plateau. The Great Sphinx in particular was the object of much veneration and was known by the name of Horemakhet ("Horus in the horizon"). Amenhotep II (c. 1454–1419 B.C.) built a temple of mud brick with limestone fittings northeast of the Sphinx, looking down on it. Amenhotep II's son, Thutmose IV, left a granite stele, known as the Dream Stele, against the Sphinx's chest, between its two paws. This text describes how the king, while one of several princes jockeying for the throne, came to hunt wild animals in the Valley of the Gazelles (as the desert at Giza was called) and took a nap in the shade of the Sphinx's head. The Sphinx came to him in a dream and asked him to remove the sand that was blanketing its body; in return it promised to make him king. So the prince had the sand removed, becoming the first archaeologist known to history as well as the first restorer. In addition, he did become king, and ruled Egypt for ten years. Of course, modern scholarship regards this inscription as, at least in part, political propaganda, designed to convince the people that although he was not the oldest son of the king, or the son of the principal queen, he had been chosen by the gods. He was thus the rightful king, pious and approved by the forces of ma'at.

The last king of the 18th Dynasty, Horemheb (c. 1343–1315 B.C.), left an inscribed monument at the site, as did the second king of the next dynasty, Seti I. Seti's son, the great Rameses II (c. 1304–1237 B.C.), was also active at Giza, and built a shrine between the paws of the Sphinx; his son and successor, Merneptah, also honored the site with a monument. Many steles were left by officials, scribes, military leaders, builders, and sculptors in honor of the Sphinx.

Other pious behavior notwithstanding, at some point before the end of the 18th Dynasty, the temples of Khafre and the Sphinx temple were systematically stripped of much of their granite and alabaster, and colossal statues weighing many tons were hauled away. This would have been a massive undertaking that must have been backed by the royal house. Someone even removed colossal granite statues from the *serdab* chambers in the Khafre pyramid temple by cutting gaping corridors more than four meters (thirteen feet) wide through more than six meters (twenty feet) of limestone core wall to reach the ends of both corridors. When did a royal house quarry Khafre's temples so carefully for stone and statues?

One section excavated along the front of the valley temple established beyond doubt that the temple was stripped of its granite sheathing before the end of the 18th Dynasty. Scattered in the one- or two-meter (three- or seven-feet) depth of sand that accumulated on the bedrock terrace were pieces of the granite facade and small fragments of statues. Mud-brick walls that rested upon this sand layer closed the main entrances to the temple. The next major layer was a villa, dating to the late 18th Dynasty, built right up against the front wall of Khafre's valley temple. The floor of the villa was 5.6 meters (18.4 feet) above the thresholds of the temple doorways, built on a foundation platform of debris fill within a grid of mud-brick walls that extended down to within 2 to 2.45 meters (7 to 8 feet) above the Old Kingdom floor—that is, nearly to the level of the mud-brick walls that closed off the temple entrances. It was clear from the stratigraphy that the facade of the valley temple had been stripped of its granite sheathing before the New Kingdom villa was built. The back of the structure was taken up by a long corridor, the west wall of which was built directly over the already-stripped limestone core blocks of the valley temple. By this point, the interior of the temple was probably already choked with sand.

In the 19th Dynasty, during the reign of Rameses II, there is clear evidence for the use of Giza as a royal quarry. Odds and ends are scattered at his building sites: a red granite block inscribed with Khafre's name was taken to Tanis, and one of the pieces of a granite cornice from Khafre's valley temple was found in the Ramesside Ptah temple at Memphis (Mit Rahina). Graffiti left in the northwest terrace walls of the Khafre pyramid by the overseer of works, May, during the reign of Rameses II also suggest that the Khafre pyramid was quarried for stone at that time. Our recent discovery of an abandoned Ramesside double statue, carved of a block of granite casing from Menkaure's complex, provides yet more evidence for this period of reuse (to put it politely). At the same time, Rameses II's son Khaemwaset visited many of the Old Kingdom monuments in the Memphite region, restoring some and leaving identifying inscriptions wherever possible.

After the gradual collapse of the New Kingdom, Giza was once again abandoned. For almost five hundred years, the stones at Giza were silent. And then, in the 26th Dynasty, about 500 B.C., Giza was brought back to life, and the cult of Khufu in particular was reestablished. Once again, there were priests of Khufu at Giza, and his cult seems to have spread throughout the country. As mentioned earlier, a small ivory statuette of Khufu, found at Abydos in the temple of the god Khenty-imentiu (a god of the underworld associated with Osiris) in Northern Upper Egypt, was most likely carved at this time. Khufu's name was also engraved upon countless scarabs and amulets during this period.

Only a century or so later, Herodotus was fed a very negative portrait of the Giza kings, especially of Khufu (known to him as Cheops). He visited Egypt in the fifth century B.C. and collected interesting stories from the guides who showed him the monuments. He was told (as he faithfully reported) that Khufu had closed the temples of the gods, forbidding the Egyptians to make offerings to any god but him. According to his guides, the Egyptians never mentioned his name with goodwill but remembered Khufu and his son Khafre as cruel tyrants. But Menkaure was remembered as a good king who disagreed with the policies of his father and grandfather, reopening the temples and once again permitting the Egyptians to make offerings to the gods. The truth of these allegations, as we have seen, is questionable, but it is possible that folk memory preserved some glimmerings of the cult changes carried out by Khufu and his sons.

In 332 B.C., Alexander the Great rode into Memphis in triumph, having just come from defeating the ruler of the Persian Empire. The Egyptians surrendered without a fight, and Alexander rewarded them by worshipping their gods and respecting their traditions. The Ptolemaic dynasty, founded by one of his generals, ruled Egypt for three centuries, until Cleopatra VII lost to Octavian in 30 B.C. One of the great contributions of the Ptolemies to our understanding of ancient Egypt was their support of Manetho, who left us a history of the Egyptian kings. It has been greatly garbled by time, and much of the information was already questionable in Manetho's own day, but its details reinforce the importance of the Giza kings, and especially of Giza, the site.

In the Roman period the area around the Sphinx became a very popular place of pilgrimage. The Sphinx then became a statue of mystery, and we know little of its history until the fifth century A.D., when Arab iconoclasts expressed their displeasure with this pagan image by breaking off its nose, leaving it with the flat-faced, beardless image so familiar to us today.

And then came the centuries of mystery and neglect, when the monuments of ancient Egypt were hidden by sand and their original meanings were lost in the mists of time. But the Giza pyramids continued to stand tall and majestic, testimony to the greatness of the kings who had built them.

Conclusion

The achievements of the house of Sneferu were remarkable. The kings ruled according to the precepts of the principle of *ma'at*, through justice and truth. These men were absolute monarchs, and their monuments bear witness to the power they held. In return, these men were solely responsible for the proper functioning of the Egyptian cosmos. In reality, the kings were dependent on the well-organized bureaucracy that supported them and on the remarkable scientists—architects and engineers—who designed and executed their monuments.

The pyramid projects were important unifying forces for the country as a whole. The workshops attached to the pyramids were in fact schools to teach arts and crafts. Workmen came from all over the country to participate in the pyramid building, bringing with them local customs and picking up the habits and styles of the capital, creating a national culture. The vast royal estates were tools for redistribution in a land where the population was dependent on agriculture and animal husbandry. Everyone involved in the pyramids or royal cults, from the workmen hauling the stones to the priests reciting the cult rites, was paid from the products of these estates; the men and women of the court were rewarded for their loyalty and excellent service from these public treasuries.

The enormous wealth held by the royal family of the 4th Dynasty is reflected in their tombs. Hetepheres I, mother of Khufu, was buried with exquisite wooden furniture and elegant jewelry. Mersyankh III, only one of a number of granddaughters of Khufu (albeit a very important one), lists in her tomb the estates available for her mortuary cult. This includes land in thirty to forty nomes.

Over time, as the family tree of Sneferu sprouted more and more branches, the wealth once concentrated in only a few hands became divided and diluted. The pyramid projects themselves, and the practice of burying a large percentage of the portable wealth of the country with its elite dead, also contributed to the drain on the royal treasuries. By the fall of the 4th Dynasty, much of the land once held by the crown had been transferred to private hands, and the power of the royal family began to decrease.

This was only one factor leading to the collapse of one of the most powerful royal houses in the history of the world. Internecine fighting and struggles over the royal dogma of the sun god Re weakened the power of the crown. The three strong brothers mentioned in the Westcar Papyrus, identified as the 5th Dynasty kings Userkaf, Sahure, and Neferirkare, were able to defeat the legendary 4th Dynasty and take the throne of Egypt.

Acknowledgments

I would like to thank the many people who helped me produce this book. I wish to acknowledge those who assisted me in my excavations of the pyramid builders at Giza, work that opened a new window into the history of the Old Kingdom. Mansour Boraik has been my right hand on this site, along with Mahmoud Afify. Many others helped as well. I also wish to thank the many people in my office who aid and support me, including Mohamed Ismail, El-Husseiny Abdel Bacier, Mohamed Megahed, and Brook Myers.

A special thanks has to be given to Trace Murphy, who met me at one of my lectures at the Metropolitan Museum of Art in New York and asked me to write this book, since the history of the 4th Dynasty had never before been written for a popular audience. Andrew Corbin has seen the book through its last stages, and I am grateful to him. I would also like to thank my assistant, Tarek el-Awady, and Martha Schwartz, who copyedited the book. And special thanks must be given to my friend and colleague Janice Kamrin, for editing this book.

Bibliography

Abubakr, Abd al-Mun'im. *Excavations at Giza 1949–1950*. Cairo: Government Press, 1953.

Aldred, Cyril. *Egyptian Art*. London: Thames & Hudson (reprint), 1985.

———. *Jewels of the Pharaohs*. New York: Ballantine Books, 1978.

Allam, Schafik. *Everyday Life in Ancient Egypt*. Cairo: Foreign Cultural Information Department, 1985.

Arnold, Dieter. *Building in Egypt: Pharaonic Stone Masonry*. New York: Oxford University Press, 1997.

Arnold, Dorothea, ed. *Egyptian Art in the Age of the Pyramids*. New York: Harry N. Abrams, 1999.

Badawy, Alexander. *The Tombs of Iteti, Sekhem'ankh-Ptah, and Kaemnofert at Giza*. Berkeley: University of California Press, 1976.

Baer, Klaus. *Rank and Title in the Old Kingdom: The Structure of the Egyptian Administration in the Fifth and Sixth Dynasties*. Chicago: University of Chicago Press, 1973.

Bárta, Miroslav, and Jaromir Krejčí, eds. *Abusir and Saqqara in the Year 2000*. Prague: Czech Institute of Egyptology, 2000.

Borchardt, L. *Das Grabdenkmal des Königs Sa-hu-re, I.-II. Leipzig 1910 bis 1913*.

———. *Denkmäler des Alten Reiches*, I (Catalogue général des antiquités égyptiennes du Musée du Caire, XCVII). Berlin, 1937.

———. *Statuen und Statuetten von Königen und Privatleuten*, I (Catalogue general des antiquités égyptiennes du Musée du Caire, LIII). Berlin, 1911.

Bothmer, Bernard. "Living Gifts from the World of the Dead," *Arts in Virginia* III. Fall 1962.

Callender, V. G. *The Wives of the Egyptian Kings. Dyn. I-XVII.* 3 vols. (Ph.D. dissertation, Macquaire University, Sydney, 1992).

Davies, Norman de Garis. *The Rock Tombs of Sheikh Said.* London: Offices of the Egypt Exploration Fund, 1901.

Dunham, Dows. "A Palimpsest on an Egyptian Mastaba Wall," *American Journal of Archaeology* 39 (1935).

———. *The Mastaba of Queen Mersyankh III.* Boston: Dept. of Egyptian and Ancient Near Eastern Art, Museum of Fine Arts, 1974.

Edwards, I. E. S. *The Pyramids of Egypt* (revised edition). New York: Penguin, 1986.

Fakhry, Ahmed. *The Monuments of Senefru at Dahshur,* vol. I: *The Bent Pyramid.* Cairo: General Organization for Government Printing Offices, 1959.

———. *The Pyramids.* Chicago: University of Chicago, 1974.

———. *Sept Tombeaux à l'est de la Grand Pyramide de Guizeh.* Cairo, 1935.

Faulkner, R. O., trans. *The Ancient Egyptian Pyramid Texts.* Oxford: Kessinger, 2004.

Firth, Cecil Mallaby, and B. Gunn. *Teti Pyramid Cemeteries.* I–II. Cairo, 1962.

Fischer, Henry George. *Egyptian Women of the Old Kingdom and of the Heracleopolitan Period.* New York: Metropolitan Museum of Art, 2000.

———. *The Minor Cemetery at Giza.* Philadelphia, 1932.

———. "Four Provincial Administrators at the Memphite Cemeteries," *Journal of the American Oriental Society* 74 (1954).

———. "Redundant Determinatives in the Old Kindom," *Metropolitan Museum Journal* 8 (1973).

Ghalioungui, Paul. *Health and Healing in Ancient Egypt.* Cairo: Dar al-Maaref, 1965.

Goedicke, Hans. *Re-used Blocks from the Pyramid of Amenemhet I at Lisht.* New York: Metropolitan Museum of Art, 1972.

Goneim, M. Z. *Horus Sekhem-Khet: The Unfinished Step Pyramid at Saqqara.* Cairo, 1957.

Goyon, G. *Les Secrets des bâtisseurs des grands pyramides: Khéops.* Paris, 1977.

Hart, George. *A Dictionary of Egyptian Gods and Goddesses.* London: Routledge, 1986.

Hassan, Selim. *Excavations at Giza,* vol. IV. Cairo: Cairo University Press, 1932.

————. *The Great Sphinx and Its Secrets: Historical Studies in the Light of Recent Excavations*. Cairo: Government Press, 1953.

Hawass, Zahi. *Hidden Treasures of Ancient Egypt*. Washington, D.C.: National Geographic, 2004.

————. *Secrets from the Sand: My Search for Egypt's Past*. New York: Harry N. Abrams, 2003.

————, ed. *The Treasures of the Pyramids*. Cairo: American University in Cairo Press, 2003.

————. *The Hidden Treasures of the Egyptian Museum*. Cairo: American University in Cairo Press, 2003.

————. *Silent Images: Women in Pharaonic Egypt*. New York: Harry N. Abrams, 2000.

————. "The Peak and Splendor of the Old Kingdom," in Francesco Tiradritti, ed., *Egyptian Treasures from the Egyptian Museum in Cairo*. New York: Harry N. Abrams, 1999.

————. *The Secrets of the Sphinx: Restoration Past and Present*. Cairo: American University in Cairo Press, 1998.

————. *The Pyramids of Ancient Egypt*. Philadelphia: University of Pennsylvania Press, 1990.

————. *The Funerary Establishments of Khufu, Khafre and Menkaure During the Old Kingdom*, Ph.D. dissertation, University of Pennsylvania, 1987.

————, ed. "Site Management and Conservation, Egyptology at the Dawn of the 21st Century," 3 vols. AUC Press, Cairo, 2003.

————. "The Discovery of the Satellite Pyramid of Khufu at Giza, Gl-d," in William Kelly Simpson, ed., *Studies in Honor of William Kelly Simpson*. Boston: Museum of Fine Arts, 1996.

————. "The Discovery of the Pyramidion of the Satellite Pyramid of Khufu [Gl-d]," in *Studies Sadek* (Varia Aegyptiaca 10/2-3 [1995]).

————. "The Discovery of a Pair-Statue Near the Pyramid of Menkaure at Giza," *Mitteilungen des Deutschen Archäologischen Institute, Abteilung Kairo* 53 (1997).

————. "The Workmen's Community at Giza," *Sonderdruck aus Haus und Palast in alten Ägypten: Internationales Symposium* 8 bis 11 April 1992. Cairo, 1996.

————. "Newly Discovered Blocks from the Causeway of Sahure," *Mitteilungen des Deutschen Archäologischen Institute, Abteilung Kairo* 52 (1996).

————. "The Great Sphinx: Date and Function," Sixth International Congress of Egyptology, vol. II. Turin, 1994.

————. "A Fragmentary Monument of Djoser from Saqqara," *Journal of Egyptian Archaeology* 80 (1994).

————. "The Passages Under the Sphinx," *Hommages à Jean Leclant*, vol I. IFAO, 1994.

————. "Recent Discoveries at Giza," *Sixth International Congress of Egyptology*, vol. I. Turin, 1993.

————. "The Statue of the Dwarf Pr-Ni-Ankhu Discovered at Giza," *Mitteilungen des Deutschen Archäologischen Institute, Abteilung Kairo* 47 (1991).

————. "Who Really Built the Pyramids," *Archaeology*, vol. 2, no. 2, 49–55 (May/June), 1999.

————, and M. Verner. "Newly Discovered Blocks from the Causeway of Sahure," *Mitteilungen des Deutschen Archäologischen Institute, Abteilung Kairo* 52 (1996).

Hornung, Erik. *Conceptions of God in Ancient Egypt*. Ithaca, New York: Cornell University Press, 1996.

Jánosi, P. *Die Pyramidenanlagen der Königinnen*. Vienna, 1995.

Janssen, Rosalind M. *Growing Up in Ancient Egypt*. London: Rubicon Press, 1991.

Jéquir, G. *Le Mastabat Faraoun*. Cairo, 1928.

————. *Le monument funéraire de Pepi II*. I–III. Cairo, 1936–1940.

Junker, H. *Grabungen auf dem Friedhof des alten Reiches bei den Pyramiden von Giza*, 12 vols. Vienna, 1929–1955.

Kanawati, Naguib. *The Egyptian Administration in the Old Kingdom: Evidence on Its Economic Decline*. Warminster: Humanities Press, 1977.

Kemp, Barry J. *Ancient Egypt: Anatomy of a Civilization*. London: Routledge, 1992.

Killen, Geoffrey. *Ancient Egyptian Furniture*. Warminster: Aris & Phillips, 1980.

Klemm, R., and D. Klemm. *Steinbrüche im alten Ägypten*. Berlin, 1965.

Lacovara, P., and C.-N. Reeves. "The Colossal Statue of Mycerinus Reconsidered," *Revue d'Egyptologie* 38 (1987).

Lauer, Jean Philippe. "Études sur quelques monuments de la III dynastie (pyramide à degrés de Saqqarah)." *Annales du Service des Antiquités de l'Égypte* 29 (1929).

————. *Le temple haut de la pyramide du roi Ouserkaf à Saqqara*. Cairo, 1955.

————. *La Pyramide à degrés*. I. Cairo, 1936.

————. *Saqqara: The Royal Cemetery of Memphis*. London: Scribner, 1976.

————. *Le mystére des pyramides*. Paris, 1998.

————. "Le probléme de la construction de la Grande Pyramide," in *Revue d'Egyptologie* 40 (1989).

Lehner, Mark. *The Pyramid Tomb of Hetep-heres and the Satellite Pyramid of Khufu*. Mainz: P. von Zabern, 1985.

————. *The Development of the Giza Necropolis: Khufu Project*. Cairo, 1985.

————. "The Giza Plateau Mapping Project," *Journal of the American Research Center in Egypt* 131 (1986).

————. "The Reconstruction of Sphinx," *Cambridge Archeological Journal* 2, no. 1 (1992).

————. *The Complete Pyramids*. London: Thames & Hudson, 1997.

Lepre, J. P. *The Egyptian Pyramids*. London: McFarland and Company, 1990.

Lichtheim, Miriam. *Ancient Egyptian Literature, The Old and Middle Kingdoms*, vol. I. Berkeley: University of California Press, 1975.

Málek, Jaromir. "King Merykare and His Pyramid," *Journal of Egyptian Archaeology* 56 (1970): 81–100.

————. *In the Shadow of the Pyramids: Egypt During the Old Kingdom*. Norman, Oklahoma: University of Oklahoma Press, 1992.

Manniche, Lise. *Sexual Life in Ancient Egypt*. London: Kegan Paul International, 1987.

Maragioglio, V., and C. Rinaldi. *L'architettura delle piramide menfite*. II-VII. Rapallo/Torino, 1963–1977.

Mariette, A. *Les mastabas de l'ancien Empire*. Paris: 1889.

Murray, Margaret Alice. *Saqqara Mastabas*, part I. London: Histories and Mysteries of Man, 1989.

Needler, W. *Three Relief-Sculptures of the Early Pyramid Age from Lisht*. Toronto, 1959.

Nour, M. Z. *The Cheops Boats*, part I. Cairo, 1960.

O'Connor, David, and David P. Silverman, eds. *Ancient Egyptian Kingship*. Leiden: Brill Academic Publishers, 1995.

O'Mara, Patrick. F. *Additional Lunar Dates from the Old Kingdom in Egypt*. California: Paulette, 1985.

Paolsen, Vagn. *Ägyptische Kunst: Altes und Mittleres Reich*. Königstein, 1968.

Perring, J. S. *The Pyramids of Gizeh*. London: J. Fraser, 1839.

Petrie, W. M. Flinders. *The Pyramids and Temples of Gizeh*. London: Histories and Mysteries of Man, 1990.

Porter, Bertha, and Rosalind L. B. Moss. *Topographical Bibliography of Ancient Egyptian Hieroglyphic Texts, Reliefs and Paintings*, vol. V: *Upper Egypt Sites*. Oxford: Griffith Institute, 2004.

Posner-Kriéger, P. *Les archives du temple funéraire de Néferirkare-Kakai. Les Papyrus d'Abusir. Traduction et commentaire.* Cairo, 1976.

Redford, Donald B., ed. *The Oxford Encyclopedia of Ancient Egypt.* New York: Oxford University Press, 2000.

Reisner, George A. *A History of the Giza Necropolis*, vol. 1. Mansfield Centre, Connecticut: Martino Publishing, 1998.

————. *Mycerinus. The Temples of the Third Pyramid at Giza.* Cambridge, 1955.

————. *The Development of the Egyptian Tomb down to the Accession of Cheops.* Cambridge, 1936.

————. "Nefertkauw, the eldest daughter of Sneferuw," *Zeitschrift für Ägyptische Sprache und Altertumskunde* 64 (1929).

————, and W. S. Smith. *A History of the Giza Necropolis II. The Tomb of Hetepheres, the Mother of Cheops.* Cambridge, 1955.

————, and C. Fisher. "Preliminary Report on the Work of the Harvard-Boston Expedition in 1911–1913," *Annales du Service des Antiquités de l'Égypt* 13 (1913).

Robins, Gay. *Women in Ancient Egypt.* Cambridge: Harvard University Press, 1993.

Roth, A. "The Organization of Cemeteries at Saqqara in the Old Kingdom. *Journal of the American Research Center in Egypt* 25 (1988).

Saleh, S. "Excavations Around the Mycerinus Pyramid Complex," *Mitteilungen des Deutschen Archäologischen Institute, Abteilung Kairo* 31 (1974).

Schäfer, Heinrich. *Principles of Egyptian Art.* Oxford: Griffith Institute, 1987.

————. *Priesterergräber und andere Grabfunde vom Ende des alten Reiches bis zur Griechischen Zeit vom Totentempel des Neuser-re* ("8. Wissenschaftliche Veröffentlichung der Deutschen Orient-Gessellschaft"). Leipzig, 1908.

————. *Aegyptische Inschriften aus den Königlichen Museen zu Berlin*, I. Berlin, 1913.

Schott, S. *Bemerkungen zum ägyptischen Pyramidenkult.* Beiträge Bf 5. Cairo, 1950.

Sethe, K. *Urkunden des alten Reiches.* Vol. I. Leipzig, 1933.

Silverman, D. "Pygmies and Dwarfs in the Old Kingdom." *Serapis*, 1969.

Simpson, William Kelly. *The Mastabas of Qar and Idu: Giza Mastabas.* Boston: Museum of Fine Arts, 1976.

————. *The Mastabas of Kawab, Khafkhufu I and II: Giza Mastabas III.* Boston, 1978.

————. *Mastabas of the Western Cemetery: Part I: Giza Mastabas IV.* Boston, 1980.

Smith, W. Stevenson. *Art and Architecture of Ancient Egypt* (revised edition). New Haven: Yale University Press, 1999.

————. *A History of Egyptian Sculpture and Painting in the Old Kingdom.* Boston: Museum of Fine Arts, 1946.

Spiegel, J. "Zur Kunstentwicklung der Zweiten Hälfte des alten Reiches," *Mitteilungen des Deutschen Archäologischen Institute, Abteilung Kairo* 36 (1966).

Stadelmann, R. "Das Drekammersystem der Königsgräber der Frühzeit und des alten Reiches," *Mitteilungen des Deutschen Archäologischen Institute, Abteilung Kairo* 47 (1991).

————. *Die grossen Pyramiden von Giza.* Graz, 1990.

————. *Die ägyptischen Pyramiden. Vom Ziegelbau zum Weltwunder.* Mainz, 1985.

Strudwick, N. "Three Monuments of Old Kingdom Treasury Officials," *Journal of Egyptian Archaeology* 71 (1985).

Swelim, Nabil. *Some Problems on the History of the Third Dynasty.* Alexandria: Archaeological Society of Alexandria, 1983.

Trench, A. "Geometrical Model for the Ascending and Descending Corridors of the Great Pyramid," *Gröttinger Miszellen* 102 (1988).

Trigger, B. G., et al. *Ancient Egypt: A Social History.* Cambridge: Cambridge University Press, 1983.

Verner, Miroslav. *Forgotten Pharaohs, Lost Pyramids, Abusir.* Prague: Academia Skodaexport, 1994.

————. "Die Königsmutter Chentkaus von Abusir und einige Bemerkungen zur Geschichte der 5 Dynestie," *Studien zur Altägyptischen Kultur* 8 (1980).

Vyse, H. *Operations Carried out on the Pyramids of Gizeh.* I-II. London, 1840–1842.

Wildung, Dietrich. "Zur Deutung der Pyramide von Medûm," *Revue d'Egyptologie* 21 (1969).

Wilkinson, R. H. "The Horus Name and the Form and Significance of the Serekh in the Royal Titulary," *Journal for the Society for the Study of Egyptian Antiquities* 15 (1985).

Index

Abd el-Al, Abdel Hafez, 123
Abu Rawash, 117
  Djedefre's pyramid complex in,
    110–13, 122
  royal court moved to, 9, 110, 163
Abusir:
  royal archives in, 159
  royal court moved to, 183, 184, 185,
    188
  royal tombs in, 66, 153, 186
Abusir Papyri, 86
Abydos:
  royal tombs in, 23, 24, 25, 74, 134
  temples in, 192
Afghanistan, lapis lazuli from, 173
Aha (Menes), first king of 1st Dynasty,
  57
Akhet-hotep, priest, 136
Akhet Khufu, 41, 68, 116
Akhmara, Prince, 152
Alexander the Great, 192
Amenemhet I, King, 46, 69, 189
Amenemhet III, King, 51
Amenhotep II, King, 3–4, 131, 189–90
Ankhetef, Prince, 135
Ankhhaf, Prince, 50, 79, 85, 96, 97, 105,
  115, 135
Anubis, 116
astronomy, 35, 58–59, 78
Aswan, granite from, 65, 173
Atet, wife of Neferma'at, 22, 30, 43, 86
Atum, creator god, 24, 34, 131–32
Atum-Re, 34

Bahariya Oasis, quarries in, 65, 173
Bastet, 118
Batrawi, Ahmed, 50
Baufre/Baufhor, Prince, 46, 82, 93–94,
  96, 138, 139
Bedouins, wars against, 19, 66
Belzoni, Giovanni, 122
benben stone, 34–35, 68
Benoît de Maillet, 5
Bent Pyramid, 19, 36–41, 50, 51
Bicheris (Baka), King, 9, 138, 139
Bonaparte, Napoleon, 6
Borchardt, Ludwig, 26–27
Boriak, Mansour, 162
Buto, temple of, 37
Byblos (port city), 19, 43, 65, 137

Cairo, building materials for, 5
Champollion, Jean-François, 6
Cheops (Khufu), 5, 192
Chephren (Khafre), 5
Cleopatra VII, 193

Dahshur:
  Bent Pyramid in, 19, 36–41, 50, 51
  capital city of, 32–33, 42
  mastaba tombs in, 44–45, 51
Debhen, government official, 152–53
Deir el-Medineh, 166
Dixon, Waynman, 77
Djadjaemankh, 46–47
Djedefhor, King, 9, 94, 95, 96, 138, 139
Djedefre, King, 94

character of, 112–13
court at Abu Rawash, 9, 110
cult of, 113
funeral of, 124
and his father's death, 73, 105, 179
names of, 109–10
pyramid complex of, 110–13, 122
reign of, 96, 112
as son of Re, 79, 109
and succession to the throne, 95,
    109–10, 138
Djehuty, feast of, 175
Djoser, King:
    first king of 3rd Dynasty, 24–25, 35
    Step Pyramid of, 1, 8, 21, 24–25, 29,
        180
    tomb of, 111
Dream Stele, 190
Du-hor (Sphinx), 131
Duwanera, Prince, 135, 152

Egypt:
    activities in, 19, 43
    agricultural cycles in, 24
    astronomy in, 35, 58–59, 78
    bread and beer as staples in, 165, 169
    bureaucracy of, 166
    censuses in, 40, 104, 158
    creation myths in, 15, 24, 35
    dwarves in, 136
    dynasties of, see Egyptian dynasties
    fortifications of, 18
    king lists of, 104, 138–39, 179, 183,
        193
    mathematics in, 60
    military in, 97–98
    nomes (divisions), 26, 98, 165
    roles of kings in, 16, 17, 35, 70,
        124–25
    roles of queens in, 14, 15
    Roman period, 193
    royal archives in, 159
    royal family wealth in, 195
    royal succession in, 14–15, 44, 94, 95,
        151, 179
    royal titles in, 92–93
    slavery in, 158
    towns of the dead in, 87
    trade with, 17–18, 19, 137
    Two Lands of, 15–16, 17, 56, 74, 118
Egyptian Antiquities Department,
    119–20

Egyptian Antiquities Organization
    (EAO), 127
Egyptian dynasties:
    0 Dynasty, 23
    1st Dynasty, 22, 23, 57, 87
    2nd Dynasty, 23, 24, 74, 87
    3rd Dynasty, 14, 22, 24–26, 28, 35
    4th Dynasty, 14–16, 17, 29, 46, 56, 79,
        87, 92, 93, 123, 124, 128, 134, 136,
        138–39, 151–52, 154, 176, 181,
        183, 184, 185, 195
    5th Dynasty, 23, 33, 70, 83, 86, 126,
        136, 144, 153, 159, 170–72, 183,
        184, 185, 186, 187, 188, 195
    6th Dynasty, 33, 70, 180, 185, 188
    12th Dynasty, 19, 46, 51, 58, 69, 81,
        189
    18th Dynasty, 190, 191
    19th Dynasty, 191
    26th Dynasty, 79, 192
Egyptian sphinx:
    form of, 111
    solar symbol of, 125
    see also Great Sphinx
Egyptology, 6, 7, 129

Faiyum Oasis, 22, 65
Fakhry, Ahmed, 36, 39
First Intermediate Period, 90, 111,
    188–89

Gantenbrink, Rudolph, 77
Geb, earth god, 15, 24
Giza:
    abandonment of, 185–93
    administrative center in, 166
    building materials gleaned from
        tombs in, 5, 111, 187–88, 189,
        190–92
    children of high officials in, 152
    core drilling in, 118
    cults in, 3–4, 10, 136, 143–46, 186,
        187, 188, 189, 192, 194
    destruction in, 79, 90, 111, 188
    foundation ceremonies in, 59–60
    Khafre's court in, 115–16, 117–32,
        133–37, 154, 159, 163
    Khufu's court in, 85–100, 159
    Menkaure's court in, 141, 144–45,
        151–54, 159, 163
    myths about, 4, 6–7
    pyramids in, 3, 8, 139, 150, 151, 182,

194; *see also* Great Pyramid; *specific kings*
  quarrying in, 65–66, 125–26, 152, 173, 191
  records of, 5–6
  scholarly studies of, 3, 6, 7, 159
  site chosen by Khufu, 1–2, 55–57, 86
  site-management program in, 7
  tomb robbers in, 3, 5, 6, 122, 187–88, 190
  tombs in, 10, 22, 86–87, 92, 94–95, 98–100, 136, 139, 161, 169, 171–72, 184
  tourists to, 4, 5–6
  workers' cemeteries in, 7–8, 154, 160, 161–63, 168, 169, 172, 189
  workers' holidays in, 175–76
  workers' lives in, 167–76
  workers' villages in, 64–66, 123, 151, 157–66
  worker system in, 159–60, 194
graffiti, 26, 191
Great Pyramid:
  completion of, 102
  construction of, 9, 57–66, 76–77, 80, 85, 159
  cult pyramid of, 64, 75–76, 102
  explorers in, 4–5, 77–78
  measurements of, 7
  modifications in, 67–68
  myths about, 4, 6–7, 158
  repairs to, 126
  theories about, 3
  unique qualities of, 73–74, 77
  workmen of, 64–66
Great Sphinx:
  beard of, 126–27
  body of, 128
  construction of, 9, 79, 125–32
  cults of, 3–4
  damage to, 126, 190, 193
  date of, 128–29
  Khafre linked to, 3, 9, 79, 128–31, 132
  location of, 129–30
  meaning of, 131–32
  photogrammetric maps of, 127
  pilgrimages to, 193
  position of, 130–31, 132
  restoration of, 7
  scientific study of, 3
  veneration of, 189–90
Greaves, John, 5

Haroun (Sphinx), 131
Hassan, Selim, 7, 182
Hathor:
  as cow goddess, 15
  cult of, 71, 102, 118, 121, 136, 146, 170–71
  as daughter of Re, 15, 34, 51, 125, 146
  as divine mother goddess, 145, 146
  music associated with, 72
  queens associated with, 51, 74, 75, 125
  statue of, 145–47
  as wife/protector of Horus, 15, 34, 51, 125, 145
Hatnub, alabaster from, 65, 72, 173
Heliopolis, 24, 34, 44, 83, 131, 140, 183
Helwan, Early Dynastic Period burials at, 50
Hemiunu, Prince, 43–44
  burial place of, 97, 98–99
  as chief architect, 1, 76
  death of, 97, 105
  estates of, 185
  as Khufu's vizier, 1, 44, 50, 55, 79, 85, 97
  as overseer, 57, 67, 76
  and site selection, 1, 55, 56
  and Sneferu's burial, 50
  statue of, 79
Henutsen, Queen, 91, 96, 135
Hepnikawes, 171, 172
Herodotus, 4, 52, 70, 81, 84, 159, 192
Hetepheres I, Queen, 14, 22, 42, 49, 89–91, 195
Hetepheres II, Queen, 93, 96, 110, 112, 134
hieroglyphs, 4, 6, 131
Hölscher, Uvo, 7
Hordedef, King, 139, 140
Horemakhet, 131, 189
Horemheb, King, 190
Hor-neb-rekhu (Khnum-Khufwy), 56
Horus:
  Hathor as wife/protector of, 15, 34, 51, 125, 145
  in Horemakhet cult, 131, 189
  Khafre as, 120, 132
  Khufu as, 56, 70, 74, 111
  as king of Egypt, 17
  king as embodiment of, 15, 16–17, 35, 56, 70, 74, 119, 124, 125, 146, 179

sacred sites associated with, 26, 27,
    102, 120
  Sneferu as, 15, 16–17, 35
  as son of Osiris, 17, 24, 34, 95
Horus falcon, 15, 16, 120, 145
Houdin, Jean-Pierre, 62
human sacrifice, 87
Huni, King, 14, 22, 26, 27
Hyskos period, 84

Ineb-hedj, capital city of, 22, 23
Intyshedu, chief carpenter, 109
Inventory Stele, 91, 129
Isis, 15, 17, 24, 51, 120
Isis temple, 129
Itysen, overseer, 168
Iunu (Heliopolis), 24

Janosi, Peter, 181
Josephus, 4
Junker, Hermann, 7

Kaihep, 171
Kakai-ankh, 169, 170
Kawab, Prince, 92, 93, 96, 110, 113, 134,
    135
Kay, 136, 150
Khaemwaset, Prince, 142, 192
Khafkhufu, Prince, 95–96, 114–15, 135
Khaf-Min, Prince, 96
Khafre, King:
  conspiracies of, 114–16
  court of, 115–16, 117–32, 133–37,
    154, 159, 163
  cult of, 185
  death of, 138, 140
  estates of, 164–65, 185
  family of, 133–36, 140, 152, 184
  Great Sphinx linked to, 3, 9, 79,
    128–31, 132
  pyramid complex of, 5, 115–16, 117–32
  and Re, 79
  reign of, 9, 95, 112, 137, 159
  reputation of, 192
  statues of, 120, 121, 130, 187
  and succession to the throne, 109,
    112, 115, 138
  temples stripped, 190–91
Khafre, pyramid harbor of, 118
Khafre Wer, 116
Khamerernebty I, Queen, 96, 133, 141
Khamerernebty II, Queen, 141, 150, 152

Khasekhemwy, King, 74
Khedhekhnu, Queen, 136
Khenmu, overseer, 167
Khentetenka, Queen, 110, 112
Khentkawes, Queen, 10, 86, 181, 182–84,
    185, 186
Khentkawes II, Queen, 184
Khenty-imentiu, mortuary god, 79, 192
Khenut, kneeling woman, 169
Khnum, protector god, 56
Khnum-Khufwy (Khufu), 56
Khufu, King:
  administration of, 97–100
  boat pits of, 72–74, 102, 148, 179
  court of, 85–100, 159
  cult of, 68, 71, 72, 75, 76, 79, 93–94,
    102, 109, 115, 132, 136, 185–86,
    192
  death and burial of, 73, 104–5, 109,
    179
  estates of, 185
  family of, 86–87, 88–96, 97, 115, 139,
    140, 151, 195
  and father's death, 48, 50, 51
  Great Pyramid of, see Great Pyramid
  and Great Sphinx, 129
  identification with Re, 68, 71, 72, 74,
    76, 78–79, 94, 102, 121, 132
  names of, 56, 111
  pyramid complex of, 1–2, 5, 41,
    64–66, 67–72, 74–76, 116, 121,
    136, 160
  reign of, 9, 44, 55–57, 104, 137, 159,
    165
  reputation of, 4, 80–84, 192
  sacred book of, 81, 84, 101–2
  sarcophagus of, 5, 105
  and succession, 45, 138
  writing a history of, 2–3
Khunera, Prince, 152
kohl, 173

Lacovera, Peter, 148
Lebanon, cedars of, 19, 65
Lehner, Mark, 7, 90, 117, 119, 130, 154,
    161, 163, 166
Libya, campaign against, 18
Lisht, 12th Dynasty pyramid at, 69, 70
lotus flower, 34

ma'at, 16, 17, 194
Mahmadien, Reis, 88

Mallakh, Kamal el-, 73
Mamun, Caliph al-, 4–5
Manetho, 81, 138, 139, 141, 193
Maqrizi, al-, 4
Mariette, Auguste, 119
Maspero, Gaston, 128
mathematics, 60
May, overseer, 191
Medjedu (Khufu), 56
Meidum:
    abandonment of, 32
    capital city of, 22, 27, 42, 85–86
    pyramids in, 27–31, 32, 41
    tombs in, 44
Menkaure, King, 135, 137
    court of, 141, 144–45, 151–54, 159,
        163
    cult of, 143–46, 181, 185, 186, 188
    death of, 142, 179
    destruction in temple of, 186
    family of, 153, 179, 183
    mortuary temple of, 147, 180, 186
    names of, 140
    pyramid complex of, 3, 86, 147–51,
        179, 181
    pyramid of, 5, 9, 139, 141–47
    reign of, 141, 159
    reputation of, 192
    statues of, 144–48
    and succession to the throne, 133,
        138, 140–41
Merer, overseer, 168
Meret, goddess of music, 72
Meretyetes I, Queen, 91, 92, 93, 96
Meretyetes II, Princess, 96
Meretyetes III (priestess), 136
Merneptah, King, 190
Mersyankh, Queen, 14, 29–30
Mersyankh II, Queen, 93, 115, 139
Mersyankh III, Queen, 93, 96, 134–35,
    195
Minkhaf, Prince, 135
Min-yuwn, Prince, 152
Mokattam formation, 56
mummification, 48–51, 87, 123–24, 134
Mycerinus (Menkaure), 5

Napoleon Bonaparte, 6
National Geographic Society, 74, 78
Nazlet el-Samman, 153
Nebma'at (Sneferu), 17
Neerpunesut, 184

Neferefre, 184
Neferhetepes, 157, 169–70
Neferirkare, King, 186, 195
Neferirkare-Kakai, 170, 184
Neferma'at I, Prince, 21, 22–23, 30, 32,
    43–44, 48, 55, 86, 97
Neferma'at II, Prince, 91, 96, 135
Nefertem/Re, 34
Nefertheith, chief baker, 157, 169–70
Neferti, Prophecy of, 45–46
Nefertkau I, Queen, 91, 96, 135
Nefertkau II, Queen, 96, 135
Neith of Sais, 24, 136, 170, 171
Nekaure, Prince, 152
Nekhbet, tutelary goddess, 15, 56
Nephthys, creation myth, 15, 24
Nesy-Sokar, priestess, 170
Netjerikhet (Djoser), 8
New Kingdom, 43, 104, 131, 189–90,
    192
Nisedjerkai (priestess), 136
Niuserre, 184, 186
Nofret, Princess, 13–14, 44, 86
Nubi, priestess, 171
Nubia:
    campaign against, 13, 18
    gold and hard stone from, 18, 65, 173
Nut, sky goddess, 15, 24
Nyankhhathor, 169
Nyankhptah, chief baker, 169

obelisks, 183
O'Connor, David, 74
Octavian, Roman Emperor, 193
Old Kingdom:
    decline of, 79, 188, 189
    palace foundations of, 43
    Pyramid Texts of, 33–34, 69
    quarrying and mining in, 173–74
    royal succession in, 14–15, 44
    sculptors in, 127
    style of, 28, 120–21
    trading relationships of, 16–18
On (Heliopolis), 24, 34, 35
Opening of the Mouth, 51, 71, 77
Orion, identified with Osiris, 78
Osiris:
    as first king of Egypt, 17
    Horus as son of, 17, 24, 34, 95
    Isis as sister/wife of, 15, 17, 24, 51,
        120
    Khentyimentiu associated with, 192

murder of, 17, 95
in the netherworld, 35
Orion identified with, 78
sacred sites of, 23, 120, 129
Seth as brother of, 15, 17, 24, 95

Palermo Stone, 18, 19, 21, 24, 37
Pepi I, King, 186
Pepi II, King, 72
Perniankhu, dwarf, 136
Perring, John, 27, 38
Petrie, William M. F., 7, 110, 123
Pettety, government official, 170, 171
phoenix (benu bird), 35
priesthood, hereditary, 188
Ptah, creation myth, 24
Ptahmerseti, overseer, 186
Ptahshepses, high priest, 153, 184
Ptah-shepsesu, overseer, 161
Ptah-Sneferu, 14
Ptolemaic dynasty, 51, 192–93
Punt, incense from, 173
pyramidology, 6–7
Pyramid Texts, 33–34, 58–60, 131–32

Rahotep, Prince, 13, 44, 86
Rameses the Great, King, 3
Rameses II, King, 142, 150, 191, 192
Ramesside Ptah temple, Memphis, 191
Raneb, King, 35
Ra-nebu ("Re of gold"), 35
Ranofer, government official, 85
Re (sun god), 34–36
    Atum associated with, 34, 131
    change in royal dogma of, 183–84, 195
    cult of, 35, 71, 76, 83, 102, 131
    feast of, 175
    Hathor as daughter of, 15, 34, 51, 125, 146
    Horus as son of, 16
    Khafre identified with, 79
    Khufu identified with, 68, 71, 72, 74, 76, 78–79, 94, 102, 121, 132
    represented by king after death, 35–36, 146
    as ruler of the gods, 34, 125
    Sneferu identified with, 35–36, 41, 51, 68, 76
    sun temples of, 83, 183–84
Red Pyramid, 39, 40–41, 48, 50, 51

Reisner, George, 7, 86, 88–89, 143, 144, 147, 149, 180, 187
Repyt-Hathor, priestess, 171
Ricke, Herbert, 130–31, 132
Roman period, 193

Sahure, King, 186, 195
Saleh, Abdel Aziz, 148, 151
Samman, Sedi Hamad el-, 153
Saqqara:
    capital city of, 22, 188
    mastabas in, 23, 25, 87, 171, 180, 186
    Step Pyramid at, 1, 8, 21, 24–25, 29, 180
Sed festival, 25, 29, 35, 37, 72, 102–4, 125
Sedyt, Queen, 91, 96
Seferka, priest, 186
Seila, pyramid at, 26–27
Sekhemkare, Prince, 136, 184
Seneb, priest, 136
Senmeru, overseer, 168
Seth, 15, 16–17, 24, 26, 95
Seti I, King, 190
Shahat, Allah, 148
Sheikh Said, 186
Shepseskaf, King, 10, 141, 143, 149, 153, 179–81, 182, 183
Shepsesptah, 152, 181
Shining Pyramid, 40
Shu, creation myth, 24
Sinai, exotic stones and precious metals from, 17, 19, 51, 65, 173
slavery, 158
Smyth, Charles Piazzi, 6–7
Sneferu, King:
    achievements of, 194
    administration of, 22–23
    court of, 22, 42–47
    cult of, 14, 20, 27, 28, 29, 37, 38, 42, 50, 51, 68, 76, 86
    death of, 48–51
    deification of, 19
    estates of, 19–20, 37
    family of, 19, 23, 32, 42, 45, 97, 115, 135, 195
    4th Dynasty founded by, 14–16, 17
    identification with Re, 35–36, 41, 51, 68, 76
    pyramids built by, 1, 9, 19, 21–22, 26–31, 36–41, 66, 110
    reign of, 18–20, 21–23, 40, 44
    reputation of, 45–47, 51–52, 81

solar worship, 34–36, 146
Soped, patron saint of mines, 51
Spence, Kate, 58
Sphinx Conservation Project, 7, 69, 78, 118, 125, 127
Stadelmann, Rainer, 40, 96, 129
Steindorff, Georg, 7
Stele of Khufu's Daughter (Inventory Stele), 91, 129
Step Pyramid, Saqqara, 1, 8, 21, 24–25, 29, 180
Supreme Council of Antiquities (SCA), 66, 78
Syro-Palestine, silver from, 173

Taylor, John, 6
Tefnut, creation myth, 24
Tgehenu, land of, 17
Thoth, god of writing and wisdom, 82–83, 84
Thutmose IV, King, stele built by, 3–4, 190
Toshka, diorite from, 173
Tura, limestone from, 65, 173
Turin Canon, 104, 141, 179
Tutankhamen, King, 116

Umm el Qa'ab, sacred site of, 23
Unas, King, 23
UNESCO, 127
Userkaf, King, 136, 153, 183, 186, 195

Valley of the Gazelles, 190
Verner, Miroslav, 183, 184
Vyse, Richard Howard, 38, 143, 149, 150

Wadi Hammamat, 93, 95, 138, 139, 189
Wadi Maghara, 19, 51
Wadjet, tutelary goddess, 56
Wahy, inspector, 169
Wall of the Crow, 64, 66, 116, 161, 163
Wenemniut, overseer, 168–69
Wepwawet, mortuary god, 72, 77
Westcar Papyrus, 46–47, 81, 83, 93, 94, 139, 189, 195

Youssef, Hag Ahmed, 73

Zawiet el-Aryan, pyramid complex at, 139